JUST ROCK IT!

HOW TO GET WHAT YOU
REALLY WANT

Sonia McDONALD

AUTHOR OF 'LEADERSHIP ATTITUDE'

Author: Sonia McDonald

Title: Just Rock It! How to get what you really want

ISBN: 9780994645227

Subjects: Personal Development – Professional Development

Registered with the National Library of Australia

Editing & design services: www.bevryanpublish.com

Disclaimer:

Contents

Testimonial

The purpose of this book is to fill you with confidence and show you the importance of being your own cheer leader. True, it is important to know that others are happy with your work, but it is even more important that you are excited and proud of your achievements, and unafraid to acknowledge them.

In the spirit of this book I have written my own testimonial: I encourage you too to take time to write testimonials to yourself when you achieve something major. Step back and observe the moment, and write something special to yourself. You will feel fabulous – and you will feel your confidence and belief in yourself growing every day.

"This book ROCKS! What I love about this book is that it is truly authentic, inspiring and honest. Sonia writes from the heart and she wants you to feel like you can rock it in your career, life and leadership. I love the questions and reflective exercises as they made me sit down and think about who I am, what I really want and why I rock it. Get this book! It will change your life."

Sonia McDonald
CEO of LeadershipHQ

About the Author

Sonia McDonald wrote this book, in short, because she's tired of watching individuals bully each other. She's also sick of people minimising their potential. Women and men all over the world have said to her, "I wish I felt more confident," or "I know what I want for my life but I'm holding myself back."

In this, her second book, Sonia urges *you* to **stop**. Stop with the excuses! Grab the proverbial bull by the horns, attack your future with gusto and *go farther than you ever dreamed*.

Sonia is CEO and Founder of LeadershipHQ, a team of specialist consultants with over 30 years' experience in organisational and leadership development, who have successfully helped companies complete multi-million dollar projects and build exceptional leaders and cultures.

Sonia, an inspirational keynote speaker, is also one of Australia's leading executive leadership coaches and facilitators. She holds a business degree in human resources and psychology, as well as a diploma in neuroscience, and has worked internationally to develop leaders and office culture in a number of diverse industries.

In 2016, Sonia published her first book, *Leadership Attitude – How Mindset and Action Can Change Your World*, and as a result of that book, she has cultivated a new wave of leadership and emerging leaders.

In *Just Rock It!*, Sonia delivers short, sharp strategies, wisdom and encouragement to help you break through fear and doubt, and create the career boost, business savvy or sense of self *you* yearn to achieve.

Acknowledgements

I want to acknowledge everyone who has supported and lifted me up over the years: My family; my beautiful daughter, Abby; my darling friends (too many to name); my LeadershipHQ team; my tribe; my peers; my associates; my mentors and coaches; my clients; my cheer squad.

A deep, heartfelt thank-you goes out to you.

You all rock—in a billion different ways.

Introduction

You've had a dream or come up with an idea—something that excites you, that really makes you think long and hard about why you're slogging away at your day job, or your night job, or whatever unsatisfying venture you've currently got going on.

You think you *might* quit everything else and tackle your idea, head on.

But you don't.

If this sounds familiar, know that I wrote this book for *you*.

However, if you've already run, whooping, from your office, whilst ripping off your tie and leaving a trail of papers in your wake, all the while shouting, *"Sayonara, suckers!"* (and most definitely burning all your bridges in the process), keep reading—you need my book even *more*. There are lots of great nuggets of wisdom in these pages for you, too.

As I travel the world, I meet so many people who are not living or creating the lives of their dreams. They doubt themselves; they're scared; they don't want to fail, put their hand up, take the risk; or they don't want to put themselves out there.

It breaks my heart. It leaves me asking, "Why?"

You're destined for more. I know you are. If you actually go for what you want, *what* is the worst that could happen?

I wrote this book because I'm so freaking *over* hearing people claim a lack of self-confidence, watching people sabotage themselves, and seeing others put people down. I am truly *over* the fact that we live in a culture and society today where it's frowned upon if we advocate for and believe in ourselves. I mean, *really*?

Again, *why*?

On my 46th birthday, I stood in a room with a group of people who were all part of a conference I was attending to help teenagers build their confidence and leadership skills. Most importantly, I was there with my beautiful 15-year-old daughter, who had been struggling with her sense of self-worth and self-belief. I was there to learn how to be a better leader and mother.

Frankly, it was the last thing I wanted to do on my birthday. Even though I live and breathe this stuff and can inspire, empower and grow leadership and leaders all over the world, I was dreading doing it with the most important person in *my* world.

I thought she would find it confronting, and agonising, and thought that her sullenness might make the entire experience most definitely *not* a walk in the park.

What I experienced and learned was unexpected. It brought back a rush of memories for me and seemed to transport me back to my pre-teen years. I began to remember the times when I didn't feel good enough, smart enough, and when I felt I had flat-out failed.

Here I was, turning 46, and I felt like my 12-year-old self all over again. Believe me, it was a humbling feeling, especially with my young daughter right next to me, experiencing the very same thing.

At the end of the seminar, though, I had come full circle. I reminded myself that I'm a smart, successful and amazing leader *and* mother who *is* good enough. And the best part? My daughter was *grinning* by the end of it, saying, "Wow, Mum. You really do this stuff all the time? That was great!"

I decided to write this book for those people who can't seem to grasp their potential, their greatness; for those who want a life where they can be the best version of themselves. These people (you!) simply need a little nudge, a little bit of support, confidence or motivation to *rock it*.

One Friday afternoon, I was walking around our local Westfield shopping centre with my daughter and a social media post on my phone caught my eye. I stopped, mid-step. (Have you ever had a feeling of unbelievable dismay wash over you? That's what happened to me.)

Someone I knew well had posted that he was tired of seeing people advocate on social media that they are the leaders of "this and that" and seem to only care about shameless self-promotion.

I couldn't *believe* it. I had a pretty good hunch he was referring to me because I do advocate (and rightly so!) that my company and I are the "Leaders of Leadership."

I took a deep breath and kept shopping. I decided to reflect over the weekend and talk to the person directly. By the end of the weekend, I acknowledged the fact that I had made an assumption (and to be honest, I'm not really a fan of making assumptions).

I called this person on Monday and asked about the post. He confirmed it was about me as well as a few others.

Again, deep breath. (It's important to breathe in instances like this so you can calm down the chemicals in your brain. I could tell at the time that mine were about to freaking *explode*.)

I replied, "That's interesting," which didn't even come close to conveying the depth of emotion I was feeling. The conversation continued for a little while with forced pleasantries on either end, and by the end of the conversation I said, "If I don't believe in myself, my work and my purpose, then who else will?"

The thing is, I see way too much of this. I work, coach, teach and meet many other people who don't believe in themselves, don't want to stand out or don't want to speak up. They say to me, *"What happens if someone finds out I am an imposter? What happens if I fail? What happens if someone pulls me down?"*

Stop caring about what other people think and stop the self-sabotage. You only live once! Who cares what others think of you? Guess what? What others think of you is none of your business.

You are unique. Go for it. Stand tall and shine. *You are YOU.*

IMPORTANT NOTE: This book is not for queen bees, tall poppies or bullies. This book is for those who want to shine and stand tall. It's for those who want to own it and *Just Rock It!*

Write down 5 ways you plan to get the most from this book—or some expectations you have for yourself by the end of this book.

1. _____

2. _____

3. _____

4. _____

5. _____

"Self-confidence is your best outfit. Rock it and own it."

1

FOCUS ON WHAT MAKES YOU ROCK

(EVERY FREAKIN' MINUTE, EVERY DAY.)

I have a quick quiz for you. Now, I don't want you to take much time to complete it. Jot down your immediate thoughts (I'm talking one-word answers, here!) within the next minute or so:

What are your talents? _____

What are your strengths? _____

What are your passions? _____

What are your goals? _____

What are your dreams? _____

If you groaned your way through my mini-quiz, or hemmed and hawed, or even if you knew each answer and scribbled down all of them in a jiffy, know this: Life is way too short not to focus on *you*. Focus on your skill set, have confidence, and work on you—every day. Then, before you know it, you'll be rocking every aspect of your life.

Simple, huh?

Maybe not.

When I ask my leaders at events or conferences, and my coaching or leadership programs, to write down what makes them different and unique, most people struggle. (I bet they wouldn't if I asked them to write down their weaknesses, which can be so frustrating to me.)

So, how do you find out what makes you unique? Why are you special? (Be assured, we all are!)

It really is simple to figure out your strengths, but it does take some work and time set aside for self-discovery.

Here are a few well-known strengths assessment tools available to you. Please note that it is important to have an expert debrief them for you if you complete them:

- 360 assessments—we have some brilliant ones!
- DISC (www.discpersonalitytesting.com)
- Myers Briggs (www.mbtionline.com)
- LSI (www.man-synergistics.com.au)
- Talent Dynamics (www.talent-dynamics.com/profile-test)
- Gallup Strengths Finder (www.gallupstrengthscenter.com)

Ask your peers, family, friends and work associates to tell you your strengths and talents as they see them.

Discover your values. What's important to you and why?

Write down a list of achievements, successes, what you love doing, what you're doing when you are at your best. What are you doing when you're in the "zone"?

And finally, surround yourself with people who have different strengths than you. They rock, too! The more aware you are of what makes you rock, the more you'll be able to help those around you rock right alongside you.

Write down 5 things that you believe others would say about you that rock:

1. _____

2. _____

3. _____

4. _____

5. _____

"What we think, we become."

— BUDDHA

2

YOUR THOUGHTS HAVE POWER

(MOST OF THE TIME, YOU ARE THE DIRECTOR.)

Thanks, Buddha. I love this quote, because it's true. Your mind is an amazing tool. You process approximately 80,000 thoughts a day, and those thoughts really do have power.

Think of your mind as a stage, and you are the director of your performance. You want to put the best actors on your stage (obviously, if you have bad actors, no one will want to buy tickets to see your play). You are the director of your mind, so you determine which thoughts should appear. Get rid of the bad ones—accept only Oscar-winning quality.

You probably know this already, but your mind loves to ruminate. Once, my boss gave me dozens of pieces of positive feedback and one piece of "developmental" feedback in my yearly review. Guess what I did?

You're right. I focused on that one piece of negative feedback. For days, and maybe even years! Can you think of a situation where you did this, too?

Why do we do it? Why not focus on the positive? Unfortunately, it's way easier for our brains to focus on threats or negatives; it's just part of our DNA. The more you focus on something, the more power it has.

You are your own thought director. The more you focus your mind on empowering thoughts and think about what makes you rock, the more confident and empowered you will be. Where attention goes, energy flows. Plus, physiologically, the more you tell yourself something, the more your brain will push those thoughts back into your limbic system and hippocampus, the emotional centre of the brain which also stores long-term memory and unconscious behaviour.

Practise saying to yourself, "I am strong, I am confident, I am amazing, I am talented at this, I can do this," and watch yourself ROCK it! It's amazing how having positive, useful and empowering thoughts can change your life.

Henry Ford, founder of the Ford Motor Company, also echoed Buddha's quote. He said, "Whether you believe you can do a thing or not, you are right."

Have you ever meet someone who says, "I'm not confident," or "I'm never on time," and sure enough, they're actually never confident, or on time, or whatever the fill-in-the-blank negative thought might be?

To modify that behaviour, say the opposite: "I'm confident" and "I'm on time," and you will be. (By the way, I'm working on the "on time" thing, too.)

Every time I'm about to speak on stage for LeadershipHQ (and I speak in front of audiences a *lot*), I only put amazing and powerful thoughts on my stage. I tell myself, "You've got this. You're going to rock it. You'll be inspirational and empowering."

And I am. I can do it every time—and mostly because I've told myself I can.

If you think you can't, you can't. I absolutely know that I can. If I can do it, you can, too!

Write down 5 thoughts that will empower you every day:

1. _____

2. _____

3. _____

4. _____

5. _____

"Comparison is the thief of joy."

— THEODORE ROOSEVELT

3

DON'T MEASURE YOURSELF AGAINST OTHERS

(JUST DON'T DO IT. END OF STORY.)

When I was 12 years old, I had a chronic fear of failure. I wanted to be the smartest girl at school and I would compare my test results with everyone. It got to a point where it caused me terrible anxiety for a number of years. Through the support and encouragement of some teachers at school, I finally got through that phase—and I finally realised I didn't have to *be* the best. I just had to give everything my all. It was a great life lesson, which served me well in the years to come.

Adam Galinsky and Maurice Schweitzer, social psychologists and co-authors of *Friend and Foe: When to Cooperate, When to Compete, and*

How to Succeed at Both, argue that social comparison is an innate human tendency.

In their book, they reference a study by Emory University scientist Frans de Waal, which showed that even monkeys compare what they have with other monkeys. De Waal trained capuchin monkeys to use stones as a form of currency, exchanging one stone for a cucumber slice. The monkeys were perfectly happy with this arrangement until de Waal started giving some (but not all) of the monkeys a sweet, juicy grape instead of the cucumber.

"Upon seeing this inequity, the monkey who was offered the regular cucumber went, well, apeshit," Galinsky and Schweitzer wrote. The monkeys who felt they lost out in this comparison became visibly upset, refusing to give a stone in exchange for the cucumber – and sometimes even throwing the slice back at the experimenter. "What this experiment demonstrates," the authors wrote, "is that our evolutionary ancestors did not evaluate their outcomes in isolation; rather, they evaluated outcomes in a comparative process."

Back when I first started my company, people would advise me to focus on what my competitors were doing.

"Why would I do that?" I thought. *"Why waste time, energy and brain space on what others are doing?"*

I don't believe in competitors anyway, so I've never spent much time worrying about what other leadership companies are doing. I focus on me, on my team, our talents, our purpose and focus on what makes our company unique.

Comparison only leads to discontent. Don't compare, and let others do their thing.

Focus on what you want and who you are, and do the things you want to do. Comparison can hold you back—and that's the last thing that should happen.

Focus on you, grab ahold of what you want, and rock it!

Write down 5 things about yourself that you can immediately stop comparing with others:

1. _____

2. _____

3. _____

4. _____

5. _____

"Failure is a bruise, not a tattoo."

— JON SINCLAIR

4

LOVE STUFF-UPS

(MAYBE NOT AT THE TIME, BUT LESSONS ABOUND.)

Nelson Mandela once said, "There is no failure; only success and learnings."

Every day, I coach and work with so many leaders who are scared of failure. It really stops them from taking risks, going for what they want, or even brainstorming to get involved with a new idea.

Some of the greatest stories of human success and exceptional leadership have come from the greatest stuff-ups.

We all know of Abraham Lincoln's success as president of the United States of America from 1860 to 1865, but his life also included some dramatic failures, including a business closure, loss of a love, a nervous breakdown, defeat in running for positions in the state legislature, and failing early runs for nomination to US Congress and US Senate.

What about author Stephenie Meyer? Before the *Twilight* series broke sales records, she faced the failure of rejection—multiple times. Meyer wrote 15 letters to literary agencies and received 14 rejections. Ouch!

Luckily, one literary agent took her on and eight publishers bid on the rights to publish the now-wildly successful series, which ultimately earned the author a place on the 2011 *Forbes* Celebrity 100 List.

Personally, I now love stuff-ups. I have learnt my greatest lessons through my mistakes. I've also had my best ideas and come up with great innovations when I have tried something that has failed. There have been times when I have also achieved something amazing or unexpected when I have stuffed-up.

For instance, I once launched a brilliant program for women in leadership and didn't check to see if the name of the program was being used by someone else. I got the materials, marketing and program designed and developed and guess what? I had to start all over again. I even received a letter from the other individual's lawyer asking me to pull everything down. I was heartbroken, and for a time, was rather down about the whole process. My excitement for the program just got ahead of me. I did the only thing I could: I pulled myself back up and started all over again. I launched a brand new (and even better!) program. I always look back on that incident as a great learning experience.

Failing is an important component of success. So many people don't want to take a risk, put their hand up or stand out because of fear of failure. Even when I fear failure, and have self-doubt, I fake it. I say over and over again that I can do it. And it works.

Go for it. Jump! Put up your hand. Ask! Say yes. Put yourself out there. What are the chances you will *actually* fail or make a fool of yourself?

Probably pretty small, right? If a friend or family member asked for your advice, wouldn't you tell them to go for it? Of course you would!

Then, why wouldn't you say it to yourself? So what if you stuff up? Who cares?

I bet you won't look back on your life and remember the stuff-ups; you'll look back and say, "I wish I had just given it a go."

Think of 5 of your own stuff-ups which resulted in teaching you your greatest lessons:

1. _____

2. _____

3. _____

4. _____

5. _____

Now write down 5 things you would really go for if you knew you wouldn't fail:

1. _____

2. _____

3. _____

4. _____

5. _____

"Define success on your own terms, achieve it by your own rules, and build a life you're proud to live."

— ANNE SWEENEY, WALT DISNEY

5
SET YOURSELF UP FOR SUCCESS

(ALL THE TIME.)

Quick, do me a favour. Take eight seconds to read the above quote again.

Let it sink in.

Now, do I really need to even write anything more for this chapter? Ha! It sure encapsulates everything well, doesn't it?

Ultimately, I think the most amazing, most wondrous thing about success is this: Each of us has a different definition of the word.

What does success mean to *you*?

To some people (and maybe this includes you), success means dominating the corporate world. Or maybe it's becoming filthy rich by age forty. Or maybe your definition of success is that you've raised really wonderful children.

Or maybe, just maybe, your definition of success can be anything you want it to be as long as you're ultimately happy and content with your life.

I'll let you in on a little secret. *My* definition of success means impacting others' lives and making a difference.

To me, significance to others refers to the positive changes you make to someone's life as a result of your influence on them. If you've made a significant difference in someone's life, no amount of money can beat that.

I truly do believe it.

A while back, I coached an incredible executive for a number of months. She was the head of human resources for a government agency and oversaw a large team. She worked really hard to coach her team, and then, out of the blue, she was made redundant. She couldn't believe it and neither could I. She was shocked, scared and devastated. She contacted me immediately.

"Just keep breathing and everything will be okay," I told her. She had to move through and accept the emotions. She was also a single mum, so losing her job was doubly heartbreaking for her. Though her company was no longer paying for her coaching program, I still continued working with her. After a few weeks and months of focus, positive mindset, connecting her with our networks and shaping up her personal branding, she got a great new job! I was so thrilled for her. That was one of my greatest experiences with success.

Okay. Since we all have different definitions of success, and we've established that being happy and content with your life contributes to your success, why not take it one step further and say that it's the *pursuit of your own planned goals and desires* that propels you toward success?

Yes! I love it. (In writing this, I'm wiggling all over in my chair because the proverbial light bulb just went off over my head.)

I've read a lot about successful people (we're talking dozens of books here) and one characteristic that drives these people's success (whether they're successful in politics, business, sports, arts, science, athletics, etc.) is that they're insanely goal-driven. I believe goals are fundamental to success.

In fact, Tom Corley, the author of *Change Your Habits, Change Your Life,* says that of the 233 successful individuals he surveyed for his book, eighty percent of them obsessively pursued both long- and short-term goals.

Quick lane change: Did you know that your imagination is one of the most powerful tools you can use to achieve your goals? Yes, the connection between neuroscience and imagination is undeniable. Your imagination causes your brain to fire up in ways that actually create new neural pathways. For example, if you imagine yourself winning a race, or saving a certain amount of money—your imagination actually propels you toward success!

Isn't that amazing?

There's one more item I'd like to mention that's invariably connected to success: Your values.

Core to your personal success is your value set. Your values will give you a strong indication of what is important to you and what success means to you.

So, what are your values? What's important to you?

Here's the catch, though: Don't confuse goals with values. Think of your values as a foundation, and your goals as the house built on the foundation.

For example, if you want to save money for a charity, that's a goal, but what's the value?

You got it. Making a difference is the value.

If you combine your values with the relentless pursuit of your goals (with a little imagination thrown in), you're seriously going to be unstoppable!

List your 5 most important values here:

1. _____

2. _____

3. _____

4. _____

5. _____

Okay, let's fire up that brain one more time. Success is within your grasp! What does success mean to you? Write it down!

1. _____

2. _____

3. _____

4. _____

5. _____

"The way to develop self-confidence is to do the thing you fear and get a record of successful experiences behind you."

— WILLIAM JENNINGS BRYAN

6

CELEBRATE THE SMALL SUCCESSES

(REFLECT ON YOUR WINS EVERY DAY.)

Sometimes we spend so much time pedaling, achieving and doing that we forget to stand still and smell the roses. We forget to take time to reflect on what we've achieved and the successes we've had.

It's easy to forget the little achievements or successes and focus on the stuff-ups or mistakes you're currently experiencing. You've stuffed-up right now? So what? Think about the great things you have done or achieved. This is what truly matters.

Trust me. When I'm on my death bed dozens and dozens of years from now (I hope!) I doubt I'll be thinking about the stuff-ups. I know I will want to remember what I've done and achieved.

Ultimately, it's those small successes that lead us up to our big moments. Think about it as a long, uphill slog to the summit of Mount Kilimanjaro, or some equally huge mountain. (We won't use Everest as an example—I've never been interested in participating in what those people have to do to get to the top of *that* mountain.)

So, let's use our imagination (a mountain is symbolic for whatever other big success you have planned for your life). Pretend your lifelong dream is to stand on the highest precipice of *your* gigantic mountain. Don't you think it would be worth every one of those knee-crushing steps and horrible blisters to see the beauty splayed out in front of you at the summit?

I hope I hear a resounding "YES!" from all of you!

Think about it. Almost every large goal you've ever accomplished in your life required you to achieve small successes along the way.

Here are some extreme examples, but examples nonetheless:

- If your goal is to become a millionaire, you need to save $1 first.
- If you're determined to shave off 45 kilograms, you have to begin with losing one kilogram at the start.
- How about getting out of debt? If you have $10,000 in credit card debt, you've got to chip away at it, a little at a time.

Again, these are extreme examples. Let's take the last bullet point, though, and consider what the small success could be. What if you have three credit cards, all maxed out. What if you completely pay one of them off? Small success?

Absolutely! Even if you still have two credit cards left, what an amazing, empowering feeling to accomplish something that's pressing heavily on you. Getting rid of one will ramp up your momentum, get your energy churning, and encourage you to squash the rest of that debt.

Have you ever heard of Dave Ramsey? If not, he's an American personal money-management expert and national radio personality. In his vast teachings, he has for many years purported that success in personal finance results from a little bit of maths and a lot of psychology.

For example, he advises his clients to never use a credit card and to pay off small bills first (to score small victories!) rather than focusing on, say, the mathematics of paying off credit cards with a higher interest rate first—especially if the balances are bigger.

Whew! Enough with the credit card and personal finance examples! They're not meant to make you feel bad about your credit cards— they're simply a way to show you that baby steps can truly make you feel like hitting the gas pedal toward achieving your big goals.

When I first wanted to become a keynote speaker, I would imagine myself on the stage, speaking in front of thousands at global conferences and my knees would turn to jelly and my self-sabotaging would take over. I knew I could do it but I had to start small. So, to build up my confidence, I would speak for free at local association groups or small events and the more I did it, the more confident I became.

Then I began speaking at much larger events and association conferences, mostly for free, just to gain more small successes and confidence. Now I love to speak, and the bigger the audience, the better! Remember to celebrate the small successes and embrace them. It doesn't matter how small or how big, they matter.

It works. I promise. Give it a whirl. Baby steps equal a big payoff down the road!

Make a list of 5 small successes you can achieve on your way to achieving your major goal:

1. _____

2. _____

3. _____

4. _____

5. _____

My major goal:

_____

_____

_____

_____

_____

_____

_____

"Confidence is the sexiest outfit you can wear."

— BLAKE LIVELY

7

CONFIDENCE ROCKS

(IF YOU AREN'T CONFIDENT, FAKE IT. YOU WILL BECOME IT.)

When I was younger, I spent all of my time studying—to the degree that I'd tell friends I couldn't hang out with them and chose studying over other social activities.

Looking back on my school years, I now realise that I consistently confused competence with confidence. I thought that if I spent all my time studying, my knowledge would automatically create a new, confident me.

Unfortunately, I was probably the hardest-working student in the school, yet still didn't feel confident.

How unfair, right?

Have you ever envisioned going back in time and having a discussion with your younger self? In addition to telling my seventeen-year-old self, "You really, really should rethink that terrible haircut," do you know what other advice I'd give?

I'd say, "Sonia, just fake it. Fake confidence."

It took me a long, long time to discover this, but faking confidence works, and believe it or not, numerous studies have proven this very fact.

For example, standing taller makes you appear more self-assured. Dressing professionally for a promotion helps you get the job. Simply smiling makes you happier.

Harvard business professor Amy Cuddy studies that exact phenomena. She investigates how people judge and influence others and themselves, and also why certain people have the confidence to take more risks, thereby landing them more business deals and job offers.

Cuddy was a university student when she suffered severe head trauma as a result of a bad traffic accident. Her IQ temporarily fell two standard deviations and she had to relearn skills she'd lost.

One of her professors knew she struggled after returning to school (a year later than her cohort of classmates) and urged her to fake feeling confident until she actually felt like she was. And it worked. Now she's a bestselling author, Harvard University professor, and is considered a leading authority on business management and social psychology.

Now, I want you to take a second to envision one person you know who exudes confidence. It could be a co-worker, a political figure, even a teacher in your child's school.

Guess what? The charismatic person you may be envisioning right now most definitely wasn't born knowing how to charm a crowd. I'd venture to say that he or she had to hone and cultivate that component of his or her character, just like Amy Cuddy had to do.

Just like I did. Just like you are going to do.

Remember, confidence is a choice. Unfortunately, it's something rarely taught in school—but think of the impact a simple class called "Fake it Till You're a Success" could have benefited you in your career! I'd venture to say it would have paid dividends for your future.

(By the way, have you ever noticed that some of those really important life lessons are never taught in school? I sure would have been more than okay with less calculus and more leadership training!)

Anyway, here are your first steps toward building your self-confidence:

1. Look in the mirror every day and tell yourself, "I am confident. I am smart. I am a success."

2. Then just rock it! You are capable of so much more than you really know, so start believing in yourself.

Make a list of things you can do or say to yourself to build your own confidence:

1. _____

2. _____

3. _____

4. _____

5. _____

"If people are trying to bring you down it only means that you are above them."

8

LET'S IGNORE TALL POPPY SYNDROME, SHALL WE?

(PUT YOURSELF OUT THERE.)

Ugh, Tall Poppy Syndrome. Have you ever heard of it?

This silly and absolutely real "disease" refers to a hostility toward high-achieving people. Symptoms include behaviours aimed at pulling people down in order to ruin their success.

Unfortunately, in my professional life, I've seen Tall Poppy Syndrome happen to others—and have been a victim myself. Very sadly, I've often wondered how many future and emerging leaders are stopped in their tracks by disparaging comments from others.

David Beckham once said, "When people criticise you, it is not a reason to give up, but to work harder and believe in yourself."

Yes! My advice? Ignore the nay-sayers. It really says more about them than it does about you. Stand tall, put yourself out there and achieve all the great things you've set your mind to achieve. Re-read Chapter 5 to remind yourself of all of the successes you have in store for your life.

Last year, I was asked to speak at a Women in Technology breakfast, and the topic was mentoring. The room was packed, and interestingly, I noticed that *none* of the women were networking. (At a session about mentoring! Go figure, right?)

After I had shared all of my thoughts on mentoring with the women, I picked up a coffee cup and spoon and indicated that I was done talking. I told the group we were going to play a networking game for the rest of the time I had with them.

The organiser of the event had the fullest reaction. "Are we ready? No!" She exclaimed. Everyone burst out laughing.

I smiled and replied, "Oh, yes, we are!" I banged the spoon against the cup and said, "Let's do some networking speed dating."

The energy in the room ramped up from there and it was a great success. (Ultimately, the organiser regretted her reaction and was thrilled that we had done it.)

A few months later, I was hosting a stand at the Christmas party for Women in Technology (the same group for which I'd given the mentoring presentation.)

I'd spent the night talking to a number of women and was absolutely exhausted. I was ready for a warm shower, a warm bed and lights out, and began to pack up early.

As I began putting my books away, a woman came up to me and said, "My name is Sandy. Were you at the breakfast a few months ago?"

I replied, "Yes, that was me," and paused my packing.

"I wanted to let you know that you changed my life," Sandy continued.

I was in shock. "How?" I asked, incredulous.

"You spoke about 'putting yourself out there' and finding a mentor," she said. "You gave me the courage to do it." Sandy went on to say that she found a great mentor and felt so much more courageous and confident.

By then, tears were streaming down my face, and the women standing beside me had been listening in awe. They said, "I bet that's why you do what you do!"

They nailed it right on the head. It's because of stories like Sandy's that I refuse to go through life and not give 110 percent!

Put yourself out there, ask for more responsibility, put your hand up, ask someone awesome to be your mentor. If you are told "no," keep going until you hear "yes!" You are in control.

And if anyone tries to pull you down, be kind and compassionate and always remember that it's about them, not you. Be you, own your actions and your life, and go for what you want!

Write down 5 ways you can put yourself out there!

1. _____

2. _____

3. _____

4. _____

5. _____

Remember, you ROCK! You've got this.

"Change the frame, and you change the game."

— SONIA MCDONALD

9

SUCCESS IS 99% ATTITUDE AND 1% APTITUDE

(YOU CHOOSE YOUR ATTITUDE 100% OF THE TIME.)

Your attitude can set you up for success or set you up for failure—there's no question about it.

We *all* deal with major life "stuff," whether we've got relationship issues, family problems, health difficulties, or glitches with money. Whatever it is, none of us is immune to small or large complications that crop up. Life *is not* smooth sailing all the time.

It's how we react to our situations that makes all the difference.

I recently read an article about an American football player named Chris Norton who, in 2010, fractured his C3-C4 vertebrae while making a tackle on a kickoff in a game at Luther College in the heartland of the United States.

The day after his severe injury, Chris awoke from surgery and was told he had a three percent chance of ever regaining movement below his neck. He spent the next three months at the world-renowned Mayo Clinic and continued three years of ongoing therapy.

His goal? To walk across the stage at his own graduation from Luther College. Five years after his injury, that's exactly what he did. He ignored the doctors' prognosis and defied his terrible odds.

Though all of this occurred halfway around the world from me, I was so moved by this story, especially when I read that in meeting others with similar injuries, Chris had noticed that many of them didn't have access to the necessary therapy equipment in order to reach their recovery goals (mostly because of medical insurance limitations).

He has since started the SCI CAN Foundation, which raises money to provide patients with neuromuscular deficiencies with the (very expensive) equipment they need.

Wow. *Wow.* What struck me most about this story is that he could have chosen to accept the doctors' prognosis and wallowed in a wheelchair for the rest of his life. Instead, he empowers others with his amazing attitude through speaking, through his foundation and through his actions.

Attitude matters.

I would not be where I am today without believing in myself and having a great attitude, either. I realised early on that I had a choice. I could choose an inner dialogue of self-encouragement and self-motivation, or I could choose one of self-defeat and self-pity. I realised that if I wanted to be successful, there was only one way I could program my mind.

Now, I must tell you, at times I have felt like I've faked a great attitude—and if you have to do that too, it's okay. It's a lot like faking confidence.

To me, a truly successful person has an attitude in which he or she believes that *anything* is possible. So put your attitude setting at "can-do" *right now*.

Let's brainstorm a few ways in which you can brew a fabulous attitude! How about through self-affirmation? Visualisation of your successful achievements? Positively interacting with others? Enthusiasm (I love that one!) and humour? You can think of more—I know you can!

Write down 5 ways in which you can rock a fantastic attitude. While you're writing them down, don't forget to set your sights on your goals!

1. _____

2. _____

3. _____

4. _____

5. _____

"There is no truth. There is only perception."

- GUSTAVE FLAUBERT

10
PERCEPTION IS REALITY

(NOT ALWAYS, BUT REMEMBER, YOU CREATE IT.)

Do you think you can agree with me on two things? Let's give them a try:

1. Reality is absolute truth.

2. All people perceive reality differently.

I'm going to sidestep a heavily philosophical debate and say that unequivocally, I believe most people can get on board with those two facts. Agreed?

Enter the concept of perception. Each individual perceives the world differently because we all have a different set of life experiences and assumptions.

In addition to *having* a certain set of perceptions, you also *create* perceptions about yourself and project those out to others all the time—whether you're aware of it or not.

For example, imagine if you showed up at your office on a Monday morning with a splitting headache, a rip in your outfit, having just battled horrible traffic, yet you cheerfully say to your receptionist, "Good morning, Mary! It's going to be a great day!"

Talk about creating a perception. Even though you actually feel like slugging someone, Mary now believes you've had a great start to your morning, and furthermore, she thinks you have an amazing attitude.

Just because you fake a certain perception, it doesn't mean you're a fraud. (Are you sensing a theme on these pages?) There's a reason! Faking it works—you truly become your best self the more you *practise*!

Before you began reading this chapter, had you given any thought to how your perceptions cloud reality?

I like to use social media as an example. Social media can stretch people's perceptions of reality like Silly Putty. If you see a post on social media, do you take it as gospel?

People, groups, organisations, companies, etc. all tend to post only good bits on social media, and usually only post photos and write things that reflect well on themselves.

For example, I know a lady who, to be quite honest, is a total grouch. She really is very unpleasant, but if a stranger landed on her Facebook page, the stranger sure wouldn't know about her un-sunny disposition, as she's posted dozens of happy, grinning photos of herself.

Always remember, what people post on social media (plus most of what you read on the internet) is not always reality. It's a…?

Perception! Right! Good job!

Ultimately, it's important to be aware of your own perceptions *and* to be conscious of the perceptions you're throwing out there to others.

Think of this, though: Everything I have said in this chapter is based on *my* perception of reality. Have you decided to absorb this chapter or take it with a grain of salt? Obviously, I hope you think deeply about it and find this stuff very interesting.

Write down 5 ways you can change your perceptions and why. Think about the ways changing your perception can help you achieve success.

1. _____

2. _____

3. _____

4. _____

5. _____

"Your vibe attracts your tribe."

–LOU FITZGERALD

11
TRIBE MATTERS

(PUT ASIDE TIME TO TAKE CARE OF YOUR PEOPLE.)

"Don't waste your time being what someone wants you to become, in order to feed their list of rules, boundaries and insecurities. Find your tribe. They will allow you to be you, while you dance in the rain."

— Shannon L. Alder

Seth Godin's book, *Tribes: We Need You to Lead Us*, is a great reminder that we all need a tribe. Human beings have gathered in tribes for millions of years—so this is nothing new, is it?

We were born to connect with others. In fact, all of us are social connection machines. What is crucial—absolutely *crucial*—for all of us to know is that who we choose to spend time with really matters. It really does.

The overarching theme of Godin's book is to think of a tribe as a group of people connected to each other, who are connected to a leader, who are all connected to an idea. In fact, thanks to the internet, it's actually easier in this day and age to create and be a part of a tribe.

Here's an interesting tribe (I tell you, there's a group out there for everyone): A group of shark attack victims has formed their own online support network, Bite Club, and it consists of almost 300 members. (Don't you think that's a clever name? And furthermore, did you know that Australia has the highest number of shark attacks worldwide, as well as a record 33 attacks in 2015? Gives me shivers.)

Anyway, I'd completely consider them a tribe. While it's likely you don't belong to this tribe unless you surf in Australia, maybe your tribe is a group of angel investors going after a small business venture. Maybe your tribe is a drinks-after-work club that gets together regularly to talk about presentation strategies for a big sales pitch. Whatever it is, Godin says that a group only needs two things to be a tribe: a shared interest and a way to communicate.

Godin's book explains that in order for tribes to be successful, they have to have purpose, as well as passionate, committed leaders who focus on the members of the tribe before themselves.

My tribe means everything to me. I only surround myself with people who truly believe in and support me. I always make sure I empower, care for, and encourage my tribe. I surround myself with people who want to see me succeed and care for, and about our vision and purpose. They are there when I need them, and I am there for them.

Time for my boat analogy. I only have people in my rowboat who want to help me row it. If certain people want to fill my boat full of holes, forget 'em.

Remember, people are in our lives for a reason, a season or lifetime. The seasonal ones? Though they may be hard to let go, like seasonal help, they're just temporary, and remember, that's okay.

What if you're still searching for your tribe? How do you do it?

Surround yourself with people who like the same things you do. Take a surfing class. Or a knitting class. Sign up for a workshop. Join the choir in your church. Ask people from work to hang out after hours—and *really* get to know them. Engage in activities that you love, and your tribe will follow.

One more little tidbit. At the top of this chapter, I wrote, "Your vibe attracts your tribe." This little saying has rung true for me for the majority of my life. The only way you can have a tribe that truly gets you is to be yourself—why would you want to be with a tribe that doesn't really fit you, that you can't fully engage with?

It's also important to surround yourself with tribe members that have similar values and ideals as you. My tribe members respect my values and have the same or similar ones; therefore, we all have great trust, integrity, compassion and respect for one another.

Yes, just like my mum said, and just like I say to my daughter, "Just be yourself!"

It really is good advice.

Now, name 5 ways you can build or help your tribe:

1. _____

2. _____

3. _____

4. _____

5. _____

"Ninety percent of everything is crap."

— STURGEON'S LAW

12
DON'T GIVE A CRAP

(YOU'VE GOT ZERO TIME FOR THAT. NONE.)

Have I got your attention? Yes? Good.

If 90 perc ent of everything is crap, then let's focus on the other 10 percent, or basically, the things you actually give a crap about.

As you may already know, I have published a book entitled *Leadership Attitude*. It was one of the best experiences I've ever had and also one of the most challenging.

As a leadership expert, you might think that writing a book about leadership would have been a snap for me. Well, it could have been — except that I got inside my own head and made it way tougher than it should have been.

After I published my book, can you guess the one question I was invariably asked? *All. The. Time?*

You got it. "How long did it take you to write the book?"

"Bloody forever!" I always wanted to shout at well-meaning folks. However, I always replied (and still do) with a serene and socially appropriate response: "Oh, a few years. I wish I knew it was going to be as easy as it was, as I would have done it sooner."

As I neared the final chapters of the book, it really was easier. Do you know why?

Because, toward the end of the book, I didn't give a crap about what people thought of it. I had been so worried in the beginning about what people would think that I developed a giant case of writer's block every time I sat down to write.

Once I decided I didn't give a crap about what others thought, only what I thought and wanted to accomplish, the words perpetually flowed from my fingertips onto the pages.

Let's switch gears, right here. (See what I did there? I wanted to change the subject, so I did! And did I give a crap?)

I'll let you answer that one.

My sister said I absolutely need to read the book *The Subtle Art of Not Giving a Fu*k* by Mark Manson. Of course, wildly intrigued by the title, I read it. (How many books has Manson sold from the title alone? Genius!)

Anyway, what resonated with me the most was the way Manson's book explains how we need the negative experiences and struggles in our lives. Sometimes I really believe we need to stop—just *stop!*—

pretending everything is perfect. Stop painting the illusion of a perfect life on Facebook and stop chronicling the 80,000 great things you have and do each day on social media. What if we *did* post our struggles and the negative aspects of our lives instead? Maybe we could more readily help each other. But when everyone pretends like everything's hunky-dory all the time, how do we do that?

Again, we need the negative parts of our lives to truly appreciate the positives. And we all need to get rid of the excess cacophony all around us—in essence, the crap.

Since we're being honest with each other (and doing away with our rainbows-and-unicorns, beautiful social media posts), let me share with you the most devastating event that happened in my life 13 years ago: my then-husband and I split up. He unexpectedly left my 4-year-old daughter and me whilst we were living in a foreign country. I never saw it coming. I spent days crying in the corner; grieving, yes—make no mistake about that.

However, this tragic day (really, it is a tiny blip if you consider the complete span of my life) ended up changing the entire trajectory of my life and channeled my future directly into a defined, positive role. It was the day I made a choice to reinvent myself and reframe my experience.

Has this ever happened to you? Has a negative experience rocked your world, but ended up being a powerful or life-changing force—for good?

So, in the spirit of being honest (see how easy it is?), there are days where I feel that building and growing an amazing business whilst being a full-time single mum is an exhausting struggle, but I get up and do it every day. Why?

Because I get to make a difference. Because there are so many positives that outweigh the negatives. Because I can grow and challenge myself. Because I can do it, and show my daughter strength of character and resilience, and prove that she can be indomitable, too.

Every day, I refuse to get bogged down by the minutiae of the day-to-day; I've simply resolved not to give a crap about the crap. In sum, I don't give a crap about people who try to put holes in my rowboat, to the thoughts that don't serve me, to the worry and stress about things I have no control over and that don't matter. The "not giving a crap" also allows me to devote my attention to the right things: My purpose in this life, the people who are important to me (especially my daughter) and the ways I can make a difference in the world.

So, it's about not giving a crap. But yes, it is also about giving a crap—about the right things. As Mark Manson states in his book, "You only have a limited amount of fu*ks to give. So you must choose them wisely."

Give it a go! Watch your world transform! Practise the art of not giving a crap—on the things that don't matter.

Don't be afraid! *You've totally got this.*

Write down 5 things that you won't give a crap about:

1. _____

2. _____

3. _____

4. _____

5. _____

"When your past calls, don't pick up, as it has nothing to say."

13

DON'T REGRET THE PAST; LEARN FROM IT

(THE PAST IS THE PAST. FOCUS ON TODAY.)

I think any therapist worth their salt would read this and applaud: The past is the past, the future is tomorrow, the present is a gift. Let the past go, learn from it and move on.

I've made mistakes and have had some extraordinary stuff-ups. I don't mean to sound totally callous, but *that's life*. In fact, life experience is a pretty awesome teacher, isn't it?

I love this quote by Abraham Lincoln: "If you have never failed, you have never lived."

However, I truly learnt some of my greatest lessons and insights from my most colossal failures.

I understand that getting over the past is way easier said than done, particularly when the failures are big ones. Here are some tips to help you over the humps:

- **Ask yourself if reliving the past over and over is actually helping you.** I get it—your business venture went bad, your best friend deserted you, you got fired—*whatever* it is—these things *hurt*. I know. I've been there. But with every ounce of compassion I have, I must ask you this: Does it really, really help you to wallow in the sadness of the past? Does it *actually* help you to say over and over, "He did this," or "She hurt me deeply," or *not*? I think you know the answer to this one.

- **Decide to stop being a victim.** I know that sounds harsh, but *you* are in charge of your own happiness. Your ex-boyfriend or ex-girlfriend, or ex-boss, or *whomever*—is not. You alone, and only you, are the captain of your ship. If you start to feel yourself blaming others for your circumstances, ask yourself why you should be letting them steer the ship. Why, *why* would you want to give someone else all that power over you?

- **Give yourself constructive pep talks.** As many times as you need to say it, stand in front of a mirror and tell yourself, "I am confident. I am smart. I am a success. I am worthy." Remember our chat about self-confidence in Chapter 7? Yeah, do that again!

- **Learn about and employ the power of forgiveness.** Forgiveness is a wonderful thing—but what it is *not* needs to be discussed as well. Forgiveness is *not* condoning something that someone did to you. Forgiveness is a way for you to release yourself from toxic people, toxic thoughts and toxic relationships. And furthermore, forgiveness officially launches you directly onto your own path toward healing. It's really a very freeing act.

- **Focus on the fact that your future could be even better and brighter if you let go of the past.**

It's so easy to keep hitting the "repeat" button. The past is what we know, so we keep replaying the loop. Maybe there's a certain comfort in it, no matter how horrific our past experience—again, because it's what we know. It's the future that can be terrifying: who knows what's around the corner?

Instead of fearing the future, though, let's put a positive spin on the possibilities. Can you imagine a future that's better than ever? Remember, cliché or not, with the right attitude, anything is possible.

Frustratingly, some mistakes seem to be easy to make over and over, even though we try our hardest to learn from the past. I've watched people (myself included) repeat the same errors. It's crucial to be self-aware, to recognise the signs and check yourself before you make that very same lapse in judgment all over again. I firmly believe you immediately begin to grow as soon as you see yourself start to err again.

Again, the number one reason you should let go of the past?

You. Can't. Change. It. That's it. That's all there is to it.

Learn from it. Believe that where you are today is where you need to be. Focus just on today and the choices you make today. They will determine tomorrow.

What are 5 lessons you've learnt from your past? How can you use them to make your future better?

1. _____

2. _____

3. _____

4. _____

5. _____

"Fill your heart with what's important and be done with all the rest."

14

LOVE THE BIG STUFF

(FOCUS YOUR TIME ON WHAT TRULY MATTERS.)

You know that book, *Don't Sweat the Small Stuff, and It's All Small Stuff*? The title pretty much sums it up.

Yep, you know it, I know it—we sometimes get too wrapped up in the minutiae. Think about the times small incidents occur and the amount of time you've spent (too much!) agonising over them.

At the end of the day, it doesn't matter that you broke your favourite mug. It doesn't matter that your slides didn't upload before your speech, because your presentation ended up amazing anyway. (Most of the time, don't things work themselves out in the long run? That's almost always been my experience, at least—whether we dwell on the small things or not!)

You know what I find fascinating?

I really enjoy observing how different people react to the very same (small) incident. For example, even in my personal life, I've observed what two different mums do when their little angels spill milk across the kitchen table:

Scenario 1: A child, Emily, happily bangs her cup on the kitchen table and watches gleefully as milk sloshes all over the tabletop. Emily's mum, cool as a cucumber, acts quickly, grabs a dish towel and says sweetly whilst mopping up, "Let's not do that again, love," to her child.

Scenario 2: A child, Eric, happily bangs his cup on the kitchen table and the same thing happens. Eric's mum leaps up from her chair as if on fire, heaves a huge sigh and sharply says, "You need to learn to be more careful!" She grabs a dish towel and wipes down the table and roughly wipes down her child as well.

Do you know how to become more laid-back about the little things?

Of course you do. You practise!

Use irritating incidents like that one (or others like it) as an opportunity to practise your reactions, and at the same time, retrain your brain to deal with emotions.

As you may already know, I'm very interested in the organ sitting right between your ears. Temperament absolutely makes a difference to how you handle irritating incidents. The frontal lobe of your brain is associated with reasoning, and on the opposite end is the amygdala, where emotions are generated. (For those of you who are super-curious, in between is the anterior cingulate, which mediates the two.)

When irritating incidents happen, think of your brain in a game of tug-of-war, with your frontal lobe tugging on one end and your amygdala on the other. In each person, one side is naturally predisposed to be utilised more than the other. Someone with a temper (any road ragers out there?) will inherently be more emotional and thus use the amygdala more than their frontal lobes in certain situations.

Let's do a brain-retraining activity. Let's go through a few scenarios and envision yourself reacting to them in a calm way. Let's start small.

What would you do if you accidentally bleached out your favourite work blouse? Think through your response to that incident. If it involves shaking in rage and throwing the bleach bottle across the room, try again. Let's visualise another one.

What if you presented what you thought was a great solution to a problem in a work meeting and everyone in the group shot it down? How would you react?

What would you do if someone was promoted over you at work? Whoa, that's a good one.

And, with that, our problems are no longer small. However, the point is, you can control your reaction, and you can practise to ensure that you have measured, acceptable reactions to incidents (large *or* small).

What if something you perceive as small happened and you couldn't stop thinking about it? Maybe it's bigger than you realise. A good way to handle it is to reflect briefly and see what you can learn from it.

Ultimately, just remember: Focus your time and buckets of energy on the big stuff, the big rocks, the stuff that really matters. If it's small, *let it go.*

Name 5 big-stuff items (not small ones!) you can focus on:

1. _____

2. _____

3. _____

4. _____

5. _____

"Vulnerability is not the same thing as weakness."

— BRENÉ BROWN

15

ASK FOR HELP

(SOMETIMES YOU NEED EXTRA HELP; IT DOESN'T MEAN YOU'RE WEAK.)

There is power in vulnerability. If there's one thing I have learnt since starting my company, it's to ask for help. When I do, my tribe couldn't be happier to lend a helping hand.

I'm also a full-time solo mother. I do find it challenging to balance my life at times.

Scratch that. Not just "at times" — *all* the time.

Even though I'm not a big fan of the word "hard," it *is*. Being a solo mum is really, really challenging. In fact, last year was one of the most difficult years of my life due to some personal issues. However, once I became unguarded and shared the struggles I'd been having, my tribe answered and rallied around me yet again.

Asking for help is a wonderful way to connect with people. Remember, we all need to feel connected—and we all need to ask for help.

Have you ever heard of Brené Brown? She's arguably the world's leading academic expert on vulnerability. She's a research professor at the University of Houston's Graduate College of Social Work and a nationally renowned speaker.

A product of a Texan/German-American upbringing, as a child she (ironically) was never allowed to express her vulnerability—*ever*. She acknowledges that she had to work to understand the value of vulnerability herself and that even led directly to a seat in a therapist's office.

In her TED Talk, she explains her research on vulnerability (which included six years of interviews, stories and focus groups) and through all of those interviews, she found a group of people she calls "whole-hearted," a group of people with a strong sense of love and belonging.

Her description of these individuals in her TED Talk were absolutely, mind-blowingly powerful. Here's what she said, verbatim, from her TED Talk:

"They fully embraced vulnerability. They believed that what made them vulnerable made them beautiful. They talked about it being necessary. They talked about the willingness to say 'I love you' first... the willingness to do something where there are no guarantees. The willingness to breathe through waiting for the doctor to call after your mammogram. They were willing to invest in a relationship that may or may not work out."

They were vulnerable *and – gasp! – it was okay.*

Boy, oh, boy, are there so many people in our society who *cannot, who will not,* do that, or what?

She also says—and this is genius—that vulnerability is our most accurate measure of courage, and when we expose ourselves, (in a relationship or even at work) we then have experiences that bring purpose and meaning to our lives.

See? When I shared my struggles with my tribe everyone banded together, and in the process, gave me a renewed purpose and allowed me to feel supported, loved and part of a nurturing environment. And I'd wager that my team members felt it refreshing that I was able to share with them—to open up as a real human being. (We've all seen the false bravado in leaders who refuse to eke out even the tiniest perception of weakness. What a tired, sad-sack act. Why do leaders feel they need to act invincible, like they have superpowers?)

I'm truly struck by the parallels between leadership and vulner-ability. I don't care who you are—every leader (every single one of you!) has some sort of vulnerability, and I believe if you're one of the good ones, you know you're vulnerable. Through that, you show courage and strength, and no matter what obstacle you face, you're more resilient because of it.

If you're in a leadership role (at home, at work, in your book club—*whatever*) can you imagine opening yourself up to your team? Can you imagine how it's possible that you and your team could emerge stronger than ever if you were to expose your vulnerability to solve a problem? Can you see how amazing things could happen?

Can you get on board? Can you expose your weaknesses to others? Can you ask for help?

Yes, yes, I think you can!

That said, write down 5 areas in your life you've identified where you can ask for help:

1. _____

2. _____

3. _____

4. _____

5. _____

"You have everything you need to build something far bigger than yourself."

— SETH GODIN

16

BUILD IT

(SET ASIDE TIME TO VISUALISE, PLAN, REFLECT AND BUILD.)

I'm always coming up with new leadership ideas or innovations, and every time I do, I can drum up images of the final result in my head.

For me, it's just like building a house—only backward. I immediately jump to putting the final coat of paint on the exterior, instead of first digging the foundation, then slowly moving to framing and putting up drywall.

To me, the architectural elements are just details, and I'm already sitting on my front porch with a Mai Tai.

I'm sure it drives my team members absolutely bonkers.

I always say, "Let's build it and see what happens. Don't let over-preparing or planning stop us from getting it done."

I remember when I wanted to start my own business. Even though I felt like an imposter, I started building it. I became the flipchart queen for nearly a year—I started writing ideas and insights for an entire year on that flipchart. I focused on areas such as marketing, products, services, purpose, mission, clients, brand and programs. In building the business, step by step, I could see it come to life, though I had no idea where it would take me.

Now, as I said, I seem to have switched gears. Instead of going through each painstaking step to arrive at a final result, I now start with the end result and work backward, but more on that in a little bit.

I'm particularly fond of this quote: "If you build it, they will come."

Have you ever seen the 1989 movie *Field of Dreams*, starring Kevin Costner? The actual quote in the movie is, "If you build it, *he* will come," but in popular culture, "he" is has been replaced by "they."

In *Field of Dreams*, Costner, a farmer from Iowa in the United States, hears a voice saying that exact line. He interprets this as instruction to build a baseball diamond in his corn field, and when he does, Shoeless Joe Jackson, a deceased baseball player, and seven other players arrive from the cornfields, and Costner's character, Ray, essentially gives them a second chance at living their dreams.

Even though Costner's character, Ray, builds the field and they come, it doesn't happen the way he intends, nor in the amount of time he intends, either. But he still does it, executes it, accomplishes it, and lives out so many individual dreams.

It goes like this: You take action, you increase your potential for your desired outcome, and the more time, thought and energy you give, the higher your probability of success.

But! There's a *big but* here!

Beware of the danger of just throwing out ideas and never executing them. If Ray hadn't acted on the voice he'd heard, he wouldn't have built the field. I've witnessed this firsthand: I've seen great, energetic people with the best of intentions never actually follow through with their brilliant ideas.

Seth Godin has said, "There isn't a shortage of ideas. There's a shortage of execution."

It's true, and it's a shame, really, and I try *very* hard not to let myself fall into that trap. My team members know the drill well and always work to pull off each idea, one by one. They're the ones framing and putting up drywall—and I'm grateful to each and every one of them for taking on those tasks.

Back to *Field of Dreams*. (If you haven't seen it, do.) The movie also teaches persistence, perseverance and passion in the face of what others cannot see or understand. (Ray's brother-in-law cannot see the White Sox players like Ray can.) So what do you do if others cannot see your vision?

Easy. You plough ahead, and fake it when necessary. For example, sometimes I say I've built a complete idea or product, even when I've only started planning it. Therefore, it's essential that I believe in myself and my team and our results—and we get to work to produce what I've promised, quickly!

Here's a great example: I met the pro-vice-chancellor of Queensland University of Technology (QUT) at a Neuroscience Summit in Sydney, as he was part of a panel on stage. Immediately after he spoke, I raced up to him and gave him my business card. I said, "I'm from Brisbane too. Let's connect!"

He smiled and said he would love to, and on a sunny Thursday morning at 9 am, he showed me around the QUT campus and we spoke about leadership at length. Suddenly, he stopped me on the way back to his office, and he was smiling. I was a touch worried, and I thought to myself, "What's he thinking?"

He said he was amazed at how passionate I am about leadership. I smiled back and agreed, and told him that I truly love my work and my purpose. (BTW, the passion chapter is coming up soon!)

He said he had a spare ticket to a QUT business leaders' awards night that evening and he wanted me to attend.

Needless to say, I couldn't turn down an opportunity like that and said I would love to go. As it happened, I sat next to the CEO of a mining company. We talked about—you guessed it—leadership, at length.

At the end of the evening, the mining CEO said to me, "Sonia, you should work with more women." He thought it would be so beneficial for us to deliver a Women in Leadership program. I thanked him for the idea and told him I would consider it.

The next day, I went back to QUT and gave the pro-vice-chancellor a thank-you gift for the invitation. He asked me about my conversation with the CEO, which I mentioned to him had centered around a women in leadership program.

He said, "What a great idea! When will you do it?"

I laughed and said, "I have to build it first."

He smiled and said he'd book the room at QUT and asked me for some dates. He encouraged me to just do it. So I did.

I built it, and it was far from perfect. However, I launched this incredible empowHER program which has evolved into something wonderful.

Just build it and they will come.

What are 5 things you can begin to envision, build and execute today?

1. _____

2. _____

3. _____

4. _____

5. _____

"Anything that gets your blood racing is probably worth doing."

17

PASSION IS CONTAGIOUS

(WAKE UP EVERY DAY AND SET YOUR ATTITUDE.)

Remember that episode of Oprah when Tom Cruise, in his excitement over his new relationship with Katie Holmes, wouldn't stop jumping on the couch? Have you ever experienced that thrill or felt like that before?

Can you name one thing you are passionate about? Think about it. One thing, that when you're doing it, makes you unaware of the passage of time?

I love so many things about my life, and speaking to groups of people is what I'm truly passionate about. When I'm on stage, I'm in heaven.

I really can't explain it. When I'm inspiring, empowering and educating leaders, I know I'm making a difference and I know that my passion shines through to others. When you are passionate about something, it's amazing to see how contagious this passion can be.

Speaking of public speaking, have you ever heard of TED talks? (I mentioned one a few chapters ago when I wrote at length about Brené Brown.) The annual TED (Technology/Entertainment/Design) event brings together the world's leaders, thinkers and innovators to speak on subjects they're passionate about – in 18 minutes or less. TEDx Talks occur around the world, using the TED format and rules.

If you watch Canadian economics professor Dr. Larry Smith's TEDx Talk, "Why you will fail to have a great career," you'll see that his talk has been viewed more than five million times—and for good reason.

He credits passion for the success you'll find in your career. What he says is simple: If you don't follow your passion, you *won't* have a great career.

Can you tell he's passionate about his work in his TEDx Talk?

Oh, you bet.

He tells humour-filled stories. He energetically paces on stage. He talks *about* passion *with* passion.

Smith has said, "People don't look for their passion because they haven't tasted it. If you've never tasted what it's like to get up in the morning and be pleased to go to work, you don't know what you're missing."

Can you imagine being so passionate about your career that you don't really care if it's a weekend or not? Can you imagine what it might be like to *not* constantly dream about retirement? Or consistently count the days until your next vacation? Pause and think about that. Can you imagine what that might be like—if you haven't found it already?

Maybe you've had an idea in the back of your head: *I've always wanted to start my own business.* Or, *I've always wanted to take care of children.* Or, *I want to use my stock knowledge to be a day trader.*

Okay! Risky ideas notwithstanding, it's time to find *your* passion.

If you and your job just don't click, I'll guarantee that watching Smith's TEDx Talk will make you feel a tad uncomfortable—but maybe it's a *necessary* uncomfortable.

Yes. If you find your passion, pursue it, and in the process, quit the pining-for-the-weekend job you might even despise, isn't it worth it?

What are you waiting for?

One more quote, from Smith's book *No Fears, No Excuses*: "When you feel passionate about your work, your workplace is not a prison that is meant to encase you until you've earned your freedom, and your work is not a means to an end. When you feel passionate about your work, you do not set rigid boundaries between work time and personal time, because the work itself is personal. When you feel passionate about your work, your talent has room to stretch and grow."

Here's a secret: too many people credit others with being "lucky enough" to have a passion and pursue it. I totally disagree. We all have a passion—and maybe you've used excuses in the past, or are too chicken to pursue it. (The "I have to grow up and get real" excuse rages rampant in cubicles throughout this country!)

A caveat: Though the conversation has morphed into this direction, passion can relate to other things, not just a career. If you have a passion for golf, pursue it. If you have a passion for writing, or crocheting, or boating—whatever it is, pursue it!

Think: Tom's excitement for Katie. Think: My love for speaking to groups. Yes, I literally jump on couches and stand on chairs when I speak. I love it.

Harness your passion and use it to drive you. Again, what are you waiting for?

Write down 5 things you're passionate about. (If you have more than 5, awesome! Good for you.)

1. _____

2. _____

3. _____

4. _____

5. _____

"Gratitude opens the door to the power, the wisdom, the creativity of the universe. You open the door through gratitude."

— DEEPAK CHOPRA

18

GRATITUDE ROCKS

(BE THANKFUL ALL THE TIME.)

I wake up every day and I am grateful. Grateful to have another day to do what I love, to be healthy and happy and to make a difference. I try to show gratitude to myself, my life and to others.

Be grateful for your skills, talents, passions, ability to make a difference, and above all else, to the people in your life. Being thankful for your talents and skills will create your ability to appreciate and focus on what makes you rock.

And isn't that the whole point of this book?

In addition to being internally grateful, don't forget to regularly bestow that gratitude on others. Friends, family, peers, your boss, clients—even your dentist! You'll be amazed at what rewards you'll reap for thanking others. I mean, how often does your physician receive a thank you note?

Write one—and then maybe he'll be more apt to allow you to make an appointment even if he has no time for anyone else! If you send a fruit basket to your financial advisor, maybe he'll be more likely to take your call—*whenever* you call.

Now, of course, it's not about showing gratitude to expect some sort of reward—it's about recognising those who truly deserve it. However, if it makes you feel good in the process, and you do receive some sort of benefit, well, that's just icing on the cake!

Two psychologists, Dr. Robert Emmons of the University of California, and Dr. Michael McCullough of the University of Miami, did a research study in which they divided participants into three groups.

The first group wrote about things they were grateful for during the week. A second group wrote about things that irritated them. The third group wrote about events that affected them (both positive and negative).

After 10 weeks, those that wrote about gratitude were more optimistic and felt better about their lives. They even exercised more and didn't have to visit the doctor as often! (Read: They were less stressed and less susceptible to sickness.)

Here's another really cool research project: Researchers at the Wharton School at the University of Pennsylvania randomly divided university fundraisers into two different groups. One group made phone calls to solicit donations like they always had.

The second group received a pep talk from the director of annual giving, who told them that she was grateful for their efforts.

During the following week, the university fundraisers who heard the gratitude message made 50 percent more fundraising calls than those who didn't hear the message.

Isn't gratitude awesome? The best thing is that when you show gratitude to others, it's also benefits you, too. Feelings of gratitude have been scientifically proven to be beneficial—they directly activate brain regions associated with dopamine, a neurotransmitter, which we all know is the "feel good" and "reward" neurotransmitter.

What if we began feeling grateful all the time?

Dopamine overload? Bring it on, I say!

And since I did bring that up, practicing gratitude is a skill that you can hone with time—and the more you do it, the more your dopamine-hungry brain may look for more ways to feel gratitude.

Need some pointers on how to express your gratitude to the people in your life? Here are some ideas:

- Skip the email or text and verbalise your thanks to your rock star co-worker.

- Write a thank-you note (already mentioned earlier, but it bears repeating.)

- Offer a helping hand to someone who needs it. (Office mate stuck with a huge, tangled project? Next-door neighbour needs help growing the grass seed on his lawn?)

- Acknowledge co-workers or employees publicly when they deserve it. Rounds of applause? It might embarrass some people, but who's really going to complain? I mean, *really*?

- Spend time with people who deserve your gratitude.

- Food and/or gifts! Always popular as a reward, always.

- Keep a gratitude journal for yourself. Write in it—and read it often. It'll do wonders for you.

Write down 5 things you're grateful for, and, if applicable, jot down how you'll express your gratitude to the people involved:

1. _____

2. _____

3. _____

4. _____

5. _____

"Perfection is boring. Getting better is where all the fun is at!"

19

REPEAT AFTER ME: PERFECTION DOES NOT EXIST

(BUT EXCELLENCE DOES.)

Be honest. Are you a self-proclaimed perfectionist?

Goodness, I hope not, because perfectionism is a confidence-killer. A big-time confidence-killer, and if you know anyone who is an obvious perfectionist, you know this for a fact. (And have you ever noticed that sometimes, perfectionists are often procrastinators, too? If they're worried about not being able to do something perfectly, they'll put it off. Really!)

Here's one of my favourite sayings: "It is my imperfections that make me perfect."

I'm far from perfect myself. In fact, here's the proof: *I can't cook.* I mean, I'm truly awful. If you asked me to make spaghetti, you'd wind up with overcooked noodles, huge chunks of ground beef (because the meatballs wouldn't turn out right) and spaghetti sauce (out of a jar, of course) spattered all over back of the stovetop. *(By the way, if you keep reading, I'll let you in on another little secret — something else I'm really, really terrible at doing.)*

To understand perfectionists a bit more, their motto could go something like this: Mistakes are unacceptable and my self-worth is dependent upon not making any, EVER.

But everyone makes mistakes.

Yes.

Therefore, what an unreachable goal it is to never make mistakes.

Exactly.

Food for thought: Perfectionism and excellent mental health do not go hand-in-hand, and perfectionism at an extreme level can be debilitating.

And unhealthy, too. Cortisol is released by your adrenal glands in response to fear or stress. Elevated cortisol levels interfere with learning and memory, lower immune function and bone density, increase weight gain, blood pressure, cholesterol, heart disease, etc.

Can the after-effects of perfectionism be linked to elevated levels of cortisol?

You bet. Not only that, but true perfectionists are at risk of depression, anxiety, eating disorders and other mental health problems.

Okay, okay, okay. If you're a perfectionist, by now you get it. You understand that it's not a good thing and if I've made you feel guilty, I'm sorry!

Let's talk about what you *can* do.

First, focus on your strengths and talents. We are all unique and different. We all have our own strengths, talents, skills, passions and weaknesses.

Second, if you are a perfectionist, modify your behavior. (I know, easier said than done, right?)

According to an article by Robert Leahy, PhD, clinical professor of psychology at Weill-Cornell Medical School, there is a kind of perfectionism called *adaptive perfectionism*, in which you still have high standards for yourself. You work hard and acknowledge that even though you miss the mark sometimes, in most cases, you can still give yourself a pat on the back for your efforts and be proud of what you accomplish.

For example, I have a colleague who most definitely puts in extra hours each weekday (and sometimes on weekends) and when she does a project well, she takes credit for it. When something goes south, however, she doesn't beat herself up over it, but as her natural adaptive perfectionist tendencies dictate, she goes back to the drawing board, puts in a few extra hours, and keeps going till she learns from her mistakes.

The power in all of this is to accept who you are and to love yourself just as you are—and that is essential.

If you read my first book, *Leadership Attitude*, I recommend reviewing the chapter on strengths. The research and neuroscience around focusing on strengths is truly compelling.

I love that I am not perfect—and so should you. Don't let perfection stop you from putting yourself out there and standing tall!

What makes you imperfect? (Oh, right, that reminds me—I was going to tell you what my other wildly imperfect characteristic is. Here goes: I tell the most awful jokes. I really, truly do.) Okay, now it's your turn!

1. _____

2. _____

3. _____

4. _____

5. _____

"People think that successful people don't feel like frauds. The opposite is more likely to be true."

— MIKE CANNON-BROOKES, CEO OF ATLASSIAN

20

THE IMPOSTER SYNDROME

(THE ULTIMATE REASON TO FAKE IT.)

When you experience a meteoric rise (or even a small, incremental rise over time) toward success, you really do sometimes need to pinch yourself to make sure it's actually happening.

And then, when you confirm that it's indeed happening, you might possibly feel like you don't deserve to be there—that you're an imposter.

Just recently, someone brought more of an awareness of Imposter Syndrome to the world.

Mike Cannon-Brookes, founder of Atlassian, an Australian collaboration software company, suffers from Imposter Syndrome. He said in his recent Sydney TEDx Talk that he's experienced this for 15 years. He asked candidly, "Have you ever felt out of your depth, like a fraud? Have you ever guessed or bullshitted your way out of a situation, petrified that someone's going to call you out?"

Yes, I have.

"It's more a fear of getting away with something," he continued in his TEDx Talk. "It's a fear of being discovered."

Yes! Yes! That's when I fake it!

(As I watched his talk, I cheered throughout and loudly agreed with his video on my iPad. Kind of embarrassing, I know.)

"Internally, you know you're not skilled, experienced or ever qualified enough to justify being there—yet you are there, and you have to figure a way out because you can't just 'get out,'" Cannon-Brookes said.

He mentioned how he had spoken to another successful CEO who also felt he didn't deserve to be in the driver's seat.

"Most days, I still feel like I don't know what I'm doing," he said.

Well, how's that for comforting? It's sort of a relief, isn't it, to know that wildly successful people are bewildered sometimes, too.

The fact that Cannon-Brookes suffers from it at all makes him that much more likeable, really. Who can resist a guy that is successful but is *that* down-to-earth? I mean, the guy wears a baseball cap every day, for crying out loud.

And the fact that he fully admits that he feels out of his league? Makes you want to give him a hug, doesn't it?

Is Imposter Syndrome a good thing? Does it keep a successful person grounded and maybe just a little bit humble?

I think so.

Cannon-Brookes said, "Successful people don't question themselves, they question their ideas and their knowledge. They're not afraid to ask for advice. They don't see that as a bad thing."

Refreshing, isn't it? It sure beats a CEO who's a total know-it-all.

Have you ever felt the unease brought on by Imposter Syndrome? Or, if you do feel it, maybe you haven't had a name for it until now. Here are some clues that Imposter Syndrome has meddled its way into your conscience:

1. You work hard. Overly hard. (So much so that you're trying to squash all feelings of inadequacy and prove your worth.)

2. You ask for validation all the time, from friends, family, your boss, co-workers—whomever you think needs to approve your work.

3. You procrastinate because you wonder if you're really qual-ified to complete a major task (Example: "I have to give a presentation at the company annual meeting... *Whaaat?*" And then you put off writing your speech because you're not sure you deserve to be the one to actually do it.)

Just remember, successful people feel the need to fake it, too—and at some point, they've likely felt the like imposters. Ultimately, do you *really* think everyone knows what they're doing all the time?

Of course not. To some degree, we're all making it up as we go along. No university degree, no previous job in an unrelated field, nothing—*nothing* can prepare you for everything you'll encounter out there.

So get going, and do the things we all know you can do. (And for the thousandth time, if you need to fake it, don't worry, we'll keep it between us.)

Name 5 things (or more or fewer!) that make you feel like an imposter. (And then, promptly remind yourself that feeling out of your depth may mean that what you're doing is unequivocally worthwhile. I mean, you could be changing the world for the better.):

1. _____

2. _____

3. _____

4. _____

5. _____

"When you stop learning, I believe you are dead."

–JACK NICHOLSON

21
KEEP LEARNING

(NEVER STOP LEARNING.)

When people introduce me as an expert on leadership, it makes me cringe.

Honestly.

I feel that even if I did have a PhD in leadership, I still wouldn't be an expert—because there's so much in this life I have yet to learn. In my opinion, if I truly am considered an expert, my brain may as well switch off and shut down immediately, because that will mean I've done it all, I've seen it all, and I don't need to learn anything else.

Now, we know that isn't true. So, to combat the uncomfortable feelings I get when I'm referred to as an expert, I call myself a semi-expert. (It also helps to combat the Imposter Syndrome, too.)

And I happily keep on learning. And guess what? I love it! I will likely never stop learning about leadership; it never gets mundane or feels like I'm stuck doing schoolwork because I am *so excited about the topic.*

Do you have a hobby or interest you can't get enough of? That you want to learn as much about as possible? Do you devour books, articles, blogs, and podcasts about the subject you love? If so, good for you!

I know a husband and wife team who have two individual and very separate interests: She loves learning about personal finance (borderline obsession here). She has an entirely different day job, but at night, she goes home and transforms into a freelance writer who writes about... what else? Personal finance.

Her husband, on the other hand, loves boating (full-on obsession in this situation!) He owns two speedboats, has restored one of them and spends every free minute on a lake near their home. He belongs to an online speedboat forum, in addition to constantly watching videos and reading about the particular brand of boat he loves.

The point is, neither he nor she can get enough of both of the topics they're passionate about. They love learning about them, and never want to stop reading, understanding, and absorbing absolutely everything they can about their interests.

I firmly believe your life is richer if you have something you're passionate about, something — whether it's SCUBA diving, knitting, traveling — *whatever* it is! — that encourages you to keep learning, always.

And how about learning for learning's sake? Even if you don't have a specific hobby you want to learn more about, why not choose something new? Never properly learnt to swim? Or kayak? Well, what are you waiting for?

By now, you've learnt a lot about me and you also know about my strong interest in neuroscience. Have you heard of neuroplasticity? If not—you're already learning something new! Great job.

Neuroplasticity refers to the human brain's ability to reorganise itself and form new connections between brain cells (neurons). Neuroplasticity occurs in the brain throughout adulthood whenever something new is learned and memorised.

Consider someone who has just graduated from university or has retired. Understandably, their cognitive skills take a hit because synaptic connections that are no longer used are actually being eliminated because they no longer need them. To combat, rewire and, ultimately, to keep your brain in tip-top shape, keep learning new things and practise them, and you'll form new neural pathways that form in response to learning— it's plasticity in action!

There are all kinds of studies that prove it, and furthermore, learning (the more complex the subject, the better—such as learning another language) offers ways to keep your mind sharp and even buffers your brain against aging.

For example, in a Swedish study which occurred at the Swedish Armed Forces Interpreter Academy, young recruits were taught a new language at a very fast pace.

They were given MRI scans before and after a period of three-month intensive study, and the researchers found that parts of these particular students' brains actually grew. The hippocampus and three areas in the cerebral cortex grew—just from pure learning.

Amazing, isn't it?

So, you see, learning isn't *just* for fun. It also contributes to overall health and life-fulfillment, as well.

What interest area, subject or passion can *you* learn (whether it's a brand new or not-so-new interest) and totally rock?

Write down 5 ways you can keep learning, and don't forget to write the contents of this book down as number 1.

1. _____

2. _____

3. _____

4. _____

5. _____

"I always did something I was a little not ready to do. I think that's how you grow. When there's that moment of 'Wow, I'm not really sure I can do this,' and you push through these moments, that's when you have a breakthrough."

— MARISSA MAYER, FORMER CEO OF YAHOO

22

BE COURAGEOUS. BE BRAVE.

(IF THEY SAY NO, KEEP GOING UNTIL THEY SAY YES.)

Courage: The ability to do something that frightens one; bravery.

Did you know that the word *courage* comes from the Latin word *cor*, which means *heart*?

When you really *go* for something, it's tough to not be daunted, especially when there's a gamble involved. However, if it's something you're sure you deserve and want with your whole heart, don't you think the results could be extraordinary?

Think with me. Examine your life and remember a time when you've done something you were terrified to do. You've been there, right?

We all have. Maybe you pitched your boss for an amazing new role, or asked a beautiful girl on a date or started a new venture.

Are you with me? Are you recollecting your memory or envisioning one in your real-life future? Great!

Now, when you were doing those daunting tasks, you know as well as I do that along with the bright, shiny possibilities of your wildest dreams coming true, there were other things that occurred as you stood in front of your boss, or the gorgeous girl, or a group of potential investors, or *whatever*: sweaty palms and pounding heart, your mind racing with thoughts of, "What if I fail? What if I'm rejected?"

I have a name for those nasty, unwanted thoughts. They're called ANTS (Automatic Negative Thoughts).

Needless to say, if I'm ever caught in a situation like this, I promptly squash the ANTS.

I wrote at length in my first book about ANTS. These negative thoughts, which quietly invade our minds like real ants on a red and white checkered tablecloth at a bona fide picnic, make a beeline for any crumb or morsel of confidence we've managed to scrounge up.

Remember Chapter 19 in this book? I mention perfectionism as a confidence-killer, but these destructive ANTS are probably worse.

I always think about wildly successful entrepreneurs and try to envision how many ANTS they probably had rattling around in their brains the instant they poised themselves to take their first giant leap. (I know I experienced this, too.)

Take Howard Schultz, the executive chairman and former CEO of Starbucks, for example.

He started out as Director of Marketing for Starbucks, and on a business trip to Milan, Italy, he noticed that coffee bars existed on practically every street and were also meeting places for friends and businessmen (plus, they served excellent espresso).

He tried persuading the then-owners of Starbucks to take it up a notch and offer up a café concept, but they didn't want to get into the restaurant business.

Schultz left Starbucks (unbelievable) and determined he needed $400,000 to open his own café.

He didn't have the money. He found investors, though, and it took him about a year to raise all he needed to open "Il Giornale," his first café.

Two years later, the original Starbucks owner sold Starbucks to Schultz for U.S. $3.8 million.

Imagine the courage Schultz had, and the ANTS he probably had to beat back when he:

1. Quit his job (his wife was pregnant with their first baby!)
2. Tried scraping up enough money to open his own Italian-inspired café.

Talk about guts. Courage. He positively *eviscerated* those ANTS.

Now, Schultz has passed on his legacy at Starbucks to a new CEO and is worth billions.

What if Schultz had let the ANTS take over his thoughts? What if he had allowed the ANTS to replace his positive intentions? What if, in turn, it impacted his physical and mental well-being and considerably damaged his potential to achieve his life goals?

Well, those delicious Frappuccinos wouldn't exist, now, would they? Or macchiatos. Or lattes. Mmmm… I'm getting thirsty.

The point is, you have to be brave. Step up to the plate, take your mightiest swing, and have courage.

You never know how far can go until you give it your best shot.

Remember, faking it goes a long way, too. (Gosh, how many times have I said that in this book? I promise you, it truly, truly does work.) Tell yourself *you can do it*, summon your courage, smash the ANTS, and amazing things could happen for you.

Write down 5 ways in which you can be courageous:

1. _____

2. _____

3. _____

4. _____

5. _____

"You only live once but if you live right, once is enough."

— MAE WEST

23

YOLO

(YOU LIVE EACH DAY AND DIE ONCE.)

Time is such an important resource. Don't waste it.

If there's one thing I could go back into the past and tell my younger self (other than just fake it more) is YOLO: You only live once.

Simple as that.

As I get older, I come to realise more and more that my life, loved ones, love, health, success, opportunities, travel (I could go on and on) really do matter most.

Life is going way too fast and it's way too short.

It's so short, in fact, that none of us has time to let fear, self-doubt, or excuses stop us from doing the things we've always wanted to do. Believe in yourself *now*.

Ask the guy or girl you've wanted to ask on a date, start that business, go for the promotion, visit your most desired, farthest-flung location.

If you have to fake it to get there, do it. Don't live with regrets.

Have you ever heard this quote? "Twenty years from now you will be more disappointed by the things you didn't do than by the ones you did do. So throw off the bowlines. Sail away from the safe harbor. Catch the trade winds in your sails. Explore. Dream. Discover."

Did you know that quote is most often misattributed to Mark Twain?

H. Jackson Brown, who wrote *Life's Little Instruction Book,* is actually the person who wrote it. (Also, this is a good lesson about not believing everything you read on the Internet.)

I happen to also love another of his aphorisms: "Be brave. Even if you're not, pretend to be. No one can tell the difference."

What have I been saying all along?! (I just want to say, I feel supremely validated right now. Ha!)

Here's another: "Make a list of twenty-five things you want to experience before you die. Carry it in your wallet and refer to it often."

Finally, Brown also wrote, "Live your life so that your epitaph could read 'No regrets.'"

How about not having regrets in your career?

Apparently, an Australia Institute study found that Australians work the longest hours in the developed world, with an average of 1,855 hours at work each year. So, then, are you making those hours count in a career that you love?

Are you finding joy in what you do every day? Are you actively shaping the career and the life you want? Would you be thrilled to death to go to the office on a Saturday?

Or will your epitaph read, "Miserable at work—felt chained to desk, so was cranky at home"?

Do you have the courage (see previous chapter about bravery) to either do something about it in your current job, or change your career and pursue your true passions?

I recently ran across a blog post by Karl Pillemer, an American sociologist and gerontologist who is the Hazel E. Reed Professor of Human Development at Cornell University. One day, he supposedly got sick and tired of writing about ageism and decided to found the Cornell Legacy Project, which has collected accounts of life wisdom from over 2,000 older Americans. (See? He found his true passion.)

Here's the sort of inspirational, amazing type of interview he gets to do all the time:

Edwina Albert, aged 94, said, "I tell people, 'Each person born has been chosen by fate from a trillion possibilities. How then can you complain of bad luck when you've won the greatest lottery of them all?' I didn't realise I was old until I was ninety years old. There's still so much to see and so much to read, and so much to learn. We should be thankful that we've had this opportunity to live."

Amen, Edwina. Amen.

Write down 5 ways you can live life to the fullest.

1. _____

2. _____

3. _____

4. _____

5. _____

"If you want others to be happy, practice compassion. If you want to be happy, practice compassion."

— THE DALAI LAMA

24
COMPASSION MATTERS

(REMEMBER, YOU'VE BEEN PUT ON THIS EARTH TO HELP OTHERS.)

It's super-easy to become wrapped up in your own life, isn't it?

Recently, I talked to another mum friend of mine who said, "I work all day, then I come home, spend time with my daughter, work some more in the late evening and finally, go to bed."

She went on to say that after months of traipsing through this exact routine, she began wondering what she had truly done for another person in the past year.

...And does taking care of kids count? Hmmm....

In our personal lives, we all know we should strive to be as compassionate as possible and really *be there* for others.

However, let's switch gears a little bit. What about compassionate leadership?

I believe that now, more than ever, we need leaders who know how to be truly compassionate, empathetic, kindhearted—whatever term you want to use, it all applies, and it's all good stuff.

You know as well as I do that there are a lot of greedy, self-serving individuals who lead the world. Why can't more people lead with their brains *and* their hearts?

What kind of results would companies attain if their leaders led with compassion?

For Pete's sake, if someone in your tribe's grandmother has just died, bake a casserole, sign a card and hightail it over to his/her house. It wouldn't kill you to show a little empathy.

I can tell you, though, that I've had employers—and co-workers, for that matter—who couldn't even *imagine* doing something like that for someone else.

In fact, in his book *Leadership BS,* Jeffrey Pfeffer, professor of organisational behavior at the Stanford Graduate School of Business, explains that many management practices have health effects as harmful as secondhand smoke. Unbelievably, his book states that negative workplace environments result in 120,000 excess deaths annually.

Yikes.

But you and I both know that there are people and organisations out there that are making a positive impact.

In fact, here's one: Ever heard of the Search Inside Yourself Leadership Institute (SIYLI)? It's an organisation that teaches people tools for compassion, empathy and wisdom so they can create a better world for themselves and others. SIYLI is run by experts in neuroscience, mindfulness and emotional intelligence—and a Google employee who wanted to change the world founded it.

Pretty powerful stuff, right? They teach executives and professionals from major corporations, and also run a blog that has given me some awesome ideas for my own leadership business! (Remember, you're never too old to keep learning!)

The SIYLI blog also linked me to a news story, which linked me to a website, and now I have a great landing spot if I need a boost of inspiration—www.wbur.org/kindworld. It's Boston's public radio station, which connects stories and podcasts about major acts of selflessness and kindness.

LOVE. IT. Check it out. You may not have a dry eye after listening to those.

One of the blog posts on the SIYLI website mentions *big kindness*—going beyond basic kindness toward our family, friends and co-workers—and doing major, major things for others that require total selflessness, such as donating a kidney to a total stranger.

Here's an example of what you might see/hear on that website: (it made me tear up when I read it—though I don't tell it *nearly* as well as the reporter who wrote it).

A mum from Florida had invited all of her six-year-old son's classmates to his birthday party, and not a single youngster showed up.

Ashlee Buratti, whose son Glenn suffers from a mild form of autism and epilepsy, was broken-hearted when Glenn kept asking, "When will my friends come?"

She turned to Facebook to post about her plight, and her local Florida community rallied. In total, about 15 children and 25 adults came to Glenn's party and brought gifts, including a bike.

YESSSS! (I did a double-fist pump when I read the article.) Acts like that are where true compassion really lies.

Okay, let's change tack again. One thing I like to talk about is something called self-compassion. I say this to my leaders a lot: "Remember, put the oxygen mask on yourself first."

Otherwise, what good are you to others if you don't take care of *you*?

Self-compassion means being kind and understanding of yourself when confronted with personal failings. Ultimately, the concept is to treat yourself just as you would treat another person who is suffering.

I don't think the concept of self-compassion had ever dawned on me before I became interested in leadership. After all, even as toddlers, aren't we preached to about being kind to everyone *else*?

Here's the deal: Don't forget to be kind to *you* so you can rock absolutely everything in your life!

Can I get a *triple* fist pump? And one more favor: Can I have you give some serious personal thought to this question:

Write down 5 ways you can be more compassionate toward yourself and others, so that you can change the world?

1. _____

2. _____

3. _____

4. _____

5. _____

"When you learn, teach. When you get, give."

— MAYA ANGELOU

25
GIVE, GIVE, GIVE

(WHAT GOES AROUND, COMES AROUND.)

Let's start off this chapter with a story—because we all know how much better stories stick with us compared to facts and figures.

Recently, I was in a busy café drinking a delicious coffee, and when I got to the cash register to try to pay, I was told that the person ahead of me had already paid for my coffee.

I found the gentleman who had paid for me and profusely thanked him, then promptly paid it forward by marching back to the cash register and paying for the *next* person's order.

I spent the rest of the day thinking about paying it forward, and started making a list of the ways I could truly make a difference. It went something like this:

1. Participate in a cleanup day.
2. Run for a charity.
3. Ask for donations instead of gifts.
4. Become someone's mentor.
5. Volunteer at an animal shelter.
6. Work *pro bono*.
7. Carry someone's groceries.
8. Leave a book behind (in the airport, in a restaurant) as a surprise to the next person.

(Speaking of books, the "pay it forward" concept helped me carry out a plan with my first book, *Leadership Attitude*. I designed bookmarks to place in all my books which ask people to pay my book forward so others will enjoy it.)

I'm blessed (cursed?) with a rampant imagination, so I imagined what my life might look like if I practiced selflessness like the above examples at an extreme level.

What if I took into my home every single orphan from an African orphanage? What if I made it my full-time job to feed the homeless in Sydney? What if I took care of all of the stray cats in Melbourne? (You see? Out of control.)

Then I thought about *this* for a long time after paying it forward: Do you think it's possible to practice selfless service all the time— without expecting anything in return? Is altruism for real?

Could I continually offer kindnesses without a cuff on the shoulder and a "Job well done, Sonia!" every time I did something for someone else?

Could I shoulder the burden of 82 cats with no help, no community service trophy and nobody rushing to compliment my good deeds, year in and year out?

All right, I realise I'm veering dangerously into a web of ridiculous examples here.

However, always curious to learn more, I googled "altruistic leadership" and found an example instantly.

Greyston Bakery in Yonkers, New York, commits itself to helping people succeed in life—as in, they're not really too fussed about employees' background or experience—and gives anyone a chance to be employed there, including former drug dealers, those with past criminal history, etc.

Here's another one: Blake Mycoskie, founder of TOMS Shoes, has built a One for One business model in which his company gives a pair of shoes to a child in need for every pair of shoes the company sells. TOMS Eyewear has also restored sight to over 400,000 individuals, and TOMS Roasting Company has also helped provide over 335,000 weeks of safe water to others… the list goes on.

Social justice as a business model. It works, doesn't it? As a consumer, doesn't it make you want to rush out and buy TOMS shoes as opposed to other brands?

I'll confess, I browsed their shoes for 45 minutes after I read more about the TOMS business model.

And it's profitable, too. Overall, publicly traded "conscious companies" consistently outperform the S&P 500 index in the US. Why?

They likely take better care of their shareholders. This is proof that giving *matters*. Caring *matters*!

Since my experience in the coffee shop, I've really made a point to wake up every day and think to myself, *"How I can make a difference in someone's life today?"*

If you research altruistic leadership more thoroughly, any good leader knows that leadership is more about others than themselves. Even if you are the CEO of your company, leading isn't about *you*. It's about your employees, your clients, your co-workers. You should be last on the priority list.

If that's a revelation to you, you may not be leading the way you should be.

Always remember, give with your whole heart without any expectations. The world is an amazing place—and after all, isn't that why we've been put on this earth? Of course, it is.

Write down 5 ways you can give, give, give!

1. _____

2. _____

3. _____

4. _____

5. _____

"Sometimes you just have to put on lip gloss and pretend to be psyched."

— MINDY KALING

26

FAKE IT UNTIL YOU BECOME IT

(ONCE YOU PRACTISE, IT'S EASY. TRUST ME.)

Have you ever needed to "make nice" with someone? At the behest of your spouse, perhaps you've been required to be sugary sweet to your mother-in law at Christmas? Or, under the power of your mum's patented icy glare, you've been instructed to be kind to your sister's decidedly horrific boyfriend at a family get-together? (Poor mothers-in-law and sisters' boyfriends. They sure do get a bad rap.)

Anyway, how did you go about doing it? Did you paste a fake smile on your face?

Sure, you did.

Did you realise that even though you were fake-smiling at your monster-in law, you probably made yourself a teensy bit happier in the process?

Let's go into the way back machine (into the 19th century) for a few seconds and think about Charles Darwin—he was the first to propose the theory that facial expressions not only reflect emotions, but also cause them.

So, what does putting a smile on your face have to do with your ability to achieve your goals? Absolutely everything! Darwin really was on to something. The neuroscience of faking it is real. It's been thoroughly researched that faking a particular facial expression causes you to feel that emotion.

What if we take it one step further and say this literally can affect the trajectory of your life? Overall, if you spend more time smiling and being positive or energetic, or if you are more often empty and grumpy, how does this affect your *life*? I know, I know, it's the tired glass-is-half-empty analogy—I get it.

But listen up. Your grumpiness could be *lethal to your success.*

Get this: In 2009 a group of psychologists at the University of Cardiff in Wales found that people whose ability to frown has been compromised by Botox injections are actually happier—because they *can't frown.*

The *why* is fascinating, and it's all down to neuroscience. The point is, your facial expressions—intentional or not, cause our brains to activate an automatic physiological response and can affect our overall attitude.

Quick biology lesson: In the brain, serotonin and other hormones act as neurotransmitters of the electrical impulses that are behind our thoughts and feelings. Our moods and our will to act are influenced by how high the levels of these various neurotransmitters are.

While it seems unreal that something so small can have such a big impact on our lives, the truth is that much of our behaviour, including how we react and are perceived by others in social situations, is influenced by these same chemicals.

Scientific research has shown that we can actually influence the number of hormones that are produced and released into our bloodstream simply by altering and changing the position of our bodies!

Therefore faking it, until you feel it is useful—truly works. If you feel depressed, upset, or even afraid, the first step to changing how you feel is to change the posture of your body. Even the simple act of smiling can be enough to turn your feelings around and help you to feel happier than you did just moments before.

Here's another study that backs it up: scientists at the Technical University of Munich in Germany scanned Botox recipients with fMRI machines while asking them to make angry faces. They found that the Botox recipients had much lower activity in the areas of the brain associated with emotional responses and reactions compared to control subjects.

One more Botox example: In 2006, Dr. Eric Finzi, a cosmetic surgeon in Maryland, injected Botox into the frown lines or forehead furrows of 10 clinically depressed women, and the treatment actually eliminated depression symptoms in nine of them and reduced symptoms in the tenth. Finzi's treatment works because facial expressions are inherently connected to the parts of the brain related to mood, and the muscles we use to frown (the area between the eyebrows) are precisely where Botox is injected.

If this isn't a ringing endorsement for Botox, I don't know what it is. (*Ha! Just kidding.*)

I suspect you know at least one person who always has a frown on their face. Does that person seem as if he or she is permanently grumpy? (I've resisted the urge to tell several people I know, "Smile. You might find your outlook on life improves." (There's a certain cashier at my local grocery store who desperately needs Botox! I don't think I've ever seen her smile.)

I have a friend, who, for the past five years, has been required to do large group presentations and meetings once a month, every month, and a lengthy training session for two days straight in the month of August. For five years, she has absolutely dreaded them. She has never felt at ease speaking in front of groups. While she loves everything else about her job, this part she absolutely hated. So, for at least one hour every month out of the year, she'd find herself nervous-sweaty and unhappy. And for goodness sake, what's the point in that?

I told her, "Fake it. Pretend you're 100 percent confident and start smiling your way through them."

She did. And her latest training session was the best she'd had in five years.

I challenge you to try that in your professional life. If you're not excited about a task you have to do for your job, smile your way through it and do it anyway. I guarantee both you and the project will come out the other end in much better shape than when you started. And maybe it can change the trajectory of your career!

Okay, I'll play devil's advocate here. Now, does all of this mean that you can avoid sadness and embrace success for the rest of your life by faking a smile?

No, probably not. A lot of researchers agree that if you're emotionally neutral, though, putting a smile on your face can tip your feelings in a positive direction.

Think of it this way: You sure have more to gain by smiling than by frowning as a general rule, right?

Right.

So, let's make another list, shall we?

Write down 5 things you're not excited about, but know you need to tackle—and can do them with a smile on your face!

1. _____

2. _____

3. _____

4. _____

5. _____

"Leadership is about making others better as a result of your presence and making sure that impact lasts in your absence."

— SHERYL SANDBERG

27

STAND TALL AND OWN IT

(DON'T EVER LET ANYONE BRING YOU DOWN.)

Let's talk about body language. In the world of faking it, this is a really important concept. If you haven't watched Amy Cuddy's TED Talk on how our bodies can shape our thinking, watch it! If you have, you know where I'm heading with this chapter and hopefully you're doing your Wonder Woman or Superman pose *right now*.

Cuddy is a lecturer at Harvard, and her TED Talk ranks second among the most-viewed TED Talks in history, for good reason—it truly rocks.

"We know that our nonverbals govern how other people think and feel about us," Cuddy says. "But, do our nonverbals govern how we think and feel about *ourselves*? If we fake it, can we change our entire attitude?"

I think, by now, you know the answer.

Before you do something that takes courage and an awful lot of faking it, Cuddy claims you should do power poses (hands in fists on hips, or double fist-pumping the air) which makes you look bigger, increases your testosterone, decreases cortisol (remember cortisol in our perfectionism chapter?) and *makes you more confident*.

I mentioned Cuddy a few chapters ago. (She's the one who got into a bad car accident and her IQ dropped two standard deviations because of it.) She also went to grad school, felt she shouldn't be there (felt like an imposter), called her adviser and said, "I'm quitting."

Her adviser said, "No you're not. Fake it."

Now she's a Harvard professor and bestselling author, among other accomplishments.

Gee, if she can do it, maybe you can, too?

Fake it until you become it.

Our bodies change our minds, our minds change our behaviour, and our behaviour changes our outcomes.

Five years ago, I worked with an especially combative client. He was the CEO of his own engineering firm and employed several engineers who worked for him. He had just had his employees do 360 reviews of his performance and he was surprised to learn that his employees believed he needed leadership training. They described him as a terrible listener, ineffective decision-maker and a master micromanager.

To his credit (though he did this somewhat grudgingly) he decided to seek me out for training. His employees were right, however. He really, really was all of those things, but observing him in his natural environment showed me that he was actually very insecure and covering up for it.

I taught him that leadership is about others. *Others, others, others.* I tried to pound that into his head at every opportunity. I was happy to know that by the end of our training sessions, he was starting to truly understand what he had done to damage his relationship with his team.

Since he actually was very insecure, I pointed out that I had noticed this and had him do the Superman power pose for a few minutes.

I'll never forget what he said after doing his power pose for me: "In my entire life, I don't think I've ever truly felt confident. Now, at least I have a tool I can use before I call a meeting to apologise to my employees."

To this day, I still wonder how he's doing.

Of all the character traits that exceptional leaders share, one of the most important is confidence. Those who can overcome obstacles and achieve peak performance for themselves and their organisations are known for being confident and upbeat. It is what fuels their resolve and determination.

Exceptional leaders can keep going and achieve their goals despite the odds stacked against them because they have such a high level of self-belief. They know that the only thing that can stop them from achieving their goals is their own self-doubt.

While a great leader may seem to overflow with confidence, the truth is that few of us are born that way. Therefore I truly embrace the concept of faking it, until you become it— it works! If you want to succeed you must first believe that you *can* and *will* succeed!

If you are feeling nervous, the simple act of standing up and pretending to feel more confident is actually a great way to tap into the power of your subconscious mind. You'll release the serotonin and other hormones that will stimulate positive feelings and give you the confidence you lack.

Before job interviews or speeches (or apologies!) I've coached countless people to duck into a toilet stall about ten minutes before their stressful task, put their hands on their hips, spread their feet wide apart with shoulders back, and stare confidently forward. I've been told it really works—that these power poses have helped people project power, confidence and control, and land them the job. (Here's a secret: I've used this technique, too.)

Amazingly, you will then start to project a higher level of confidence and sureness that others will mirror back to you as you interact with them. This creates what is known as a positive feedback loop, a perpetual positive energy engine that continues to increase production of the very neurotransmitters behind the feelings of positive self-worth and well-being!

Think you can employ your power poses prior to your next stressful event?

Yes, you can!

Can you stare down the obstacles that stand in your way and believe you will succeed in your quest if you believe in yourself?

Yes, you can!

Write down 5 scenarios in which you can use the Wonder Woman or Superman pose in real life. (Are you practising?)

1. _____

2. _____

3. _____

4. _____

5. _____

"It took me a long time to develop a voice, and now that I have it, I'm not going to be silent."

— MADELEINE ALBRIGHT

28

FIND YOUR VOICE

(SHOUT FROM THE ROOFTOPS.)

As soon as I thought about the topic for this chapter, I thought, "Hmmm... how many people are actually willing to sit around and think about whether they've found their *voice*?"

Yes, who has time for that? Between your job, taking care of kids/dogs/chinchillas/whatever, trying to put a decent meal on the table, spending time with family and friends, laundry, dishes, and doing everything else in between, it's kind of like, "Seriously? My *voice*?"

I hear you, I hear you. Anyway, I'll put this all together for you in a nutshell:

1. Finding your voice is really, really important—it helps you *define who you are.*

2. Only after finding your own voice can you successfully lead others.

Do I have your attention now? I hope so.

In the last chapter, we talked a lot about power poses and how they help us become confident in ourselves. I wholeheartedly believe that developing confidence is the key to cultivating your voice.

If you find your inner confidence, you'll be able to develop your natural gifts and engage in work that uses your talents. In turn, you'll fuel your passions and become absolutely unstoppable!

This stuff gets me so excited, and it also reminds me of my friend Melanie's story—I mentioned Mel and her husband briefly in another chapter.

Melanie had been working for a non-profit organisation for about ten years and ultimately realised, "I'm not good at this, and I'm not enjoying it, either. Why am I killing myself to wake up at five o'clock in the morning every day?" She realised that her freelance writing side jobs were far more satisfying to her than her actual job. (She'd been spending every lunch hour working on her freelancing jobs, anyway.)

So she bravely quit her day job (she had to do a few power poses in the process), kept freelancing, and then eventually began her own publishing firm. She's a raging success in her own right and employs several other successful agents.

Undoubtedly, Melanie found her voice.

Okay, now it's your turn. What do you really love to do? What is your natural talent? What really interests you? What if you took a critical look at your life's work and asked yourself, "Do I understand myself? Am I completely comfortable with who I am? Am I doing *what I'm meant to do*?" (Scary, I know.)

Most leadership junkies have heard of the late Stephen R. Covey's *The 7 Habits of Highly Effective People.* If you haven't, I highly encourage reading it soon. In Covey's book *The 8th Habit*, he explains how leadership greatness is all about finding your voice. He encourages you to make sure that your body, mind, heart and spirit are all engaged in what is important to you, and once you've found your voice, you can turn around and help others find theirs.

Isn't this "voice" stuff a really great analogy for leadership?

I feel extremely fortunate to be able to help people find their voices *every day*. To me, this is akin to being an obstetrician and delivering tiny miracles all the time. People (you) have so much leadership potential; it's truly amazing!

Have I worked with people who aren't in the right field? Have I worked with people who aren't developing the right set of talents for themselves?

You bet, and that can be a hard, terrifying reality to swallow. But you know what? It can also be the most liberating.

I've actually said this to a 35-year-old professional: "You know, I just don't think sales and marketing is the right field for you. Instead, I think your strengths lie in event planning. Wow, you'd shine there."

The woman I gave that advice to promptly burst into tears. She said, "Sonia, I've never felt at ease at work. I'm just not good at marketing. I like things to be structured, orderly and I think you're exactly right."

Within weeks, she obtained a different position within her company and the last time I checked, she was happily using her innate talents to organise a major conference and also had a few interns under her tutelage. (I marveled at seeing her do that—she was inspiring others to find their voices. The 8th habit, in action. Wow!)

Remember this well: In order to add lasting impact—real, meaningful value to your workplace, your profession, your life—you must first find your own voice.

Only after you've accomplished that can you lead others, and lead them well.

If you haven't already found it, write down 5 steps you can take to help you find your voice. If you have found your voice, write down 5 things you can do to help others find theirs:

1. _____

2. _____

3. _____

4. _____

5. _____

"A lot of people put pressure on themselves and think it will be way too hard for them to live out their dreams. Mentors are there to say, 'Look, it's not that tough. It's not as hard as you think. Here are some guidelines and things I have gone through to get where I am in my career.'"

— JOE JONAS

29

GET A COACH OR MENTOR TO HELP YOU BECOME IT

(IT'LL CHANGE YOUR LIFE.)

Almost every wildly successful person in the world had a great mentor.

Tim Ferriss (author of the *Four Hour Work Week*) was mentored by *Chicken Soup for the Soul* author Jack Canfield.

A few more:

- Poet Maya Angelou mentored American media proprietor Oprah Winfrey.
- Steve Jobs mentored Mark Zuckerberg.

- Warren Buffett mentored Bill Gates.
- Ralph Waldo Emerson mentored Henry David Thoreau.

So, now, why not you…and someone else? If you currently have a mentor, good for you. If you don't, why aren't you working on getting one *right now*?

In a leadership seminar that I led a few weeks ago, I mentioned to the audience that having a mentor is a wonderful thing. Eight seconds after I said it, someone raised his hand and said, "Sonia, I just want to play devil's advocate here. I'm doing pretty well for myself right now. Why do I need a mentor?"

I punched the air with my finger. "I'm so glad you asked that question!" I bounded over to him and asked him his name. He said it was Kyle.

"Okay, Kyle, what if you found a mentor who was able to stimulate your professional growth? What if they could see areas you need to improve that you can't see? What if they connect you to others in your field? What if they, providing a *free service*, elevate your career in a way you'd never have thought possible?" I paused, then said, "What if they can help you *fake it*?"

Kyle sat, thinking, then said, "So I can't afford *not* to have a mentor."

"Right. It's like saving for retirement. You can't afford *not* to do it," I told him.

I went on to advise Kyle and the rest of the remarkable people in that seminar to not approach a potential mentor who is a stranger. It's much easier to find mentors through the people you're already interacting with now, because they already know you and can make the leap to trusting and seeing the potential in you (otherwise, why would they want to mentor you?)

Here are some good ideas for getting started:

1. Be mentor-worthy. Be honest with yourself. Would *you* want to mentor you? Are you a rising star in your field? If not, why would your potential mentor want to mentor you? (How many times can I say the word "mentor"? Mentor, mentor, mentor.)

2. Gently ask this person (whom you already know) to be your mentor. And if you have identified someone who doesn't know you, let them get to know you before you ask. Volunteer to help them with a project they have going on, or ask for advice on one of your own projects, if they work at the same workplace as you.

3. Engage, follow up, be likeable. And reciprocal. When you meet with your mentor, be professional, ask great questions (not ones that can be googled!) and be sure to nurture the relationship.

4. Again, be worth mentoring! (I don't think I can say that enough.)

I've had astounding mentors and coaches on my side over the years. Much like Harvard professor Amy Cuddy and her graduate school adviser, who refused to accept Cuddy's decision to quit, said to her, "No, you're not quitting. Fake it." I've also had mentors who have pushed me to succeed and helped me see the potential I couldn't see in myself.

And you know, I get my knocks. I am not Ms Confident 24/7. The thing is, when I look on everything I've done—the learnings, stuff-ups, plus my successes and achievements, the one thing that made the greatest difference was finding my mentors and coaches.

And when you do encounter "the crazy" in your career or your life, it's your mentor (if you have a good one) who will pull you up and patch you back together.

Write down 5 people you can think of who could be a coach or mentor for you, and how you'll approach asking for their mentorship.

1. _____

2. _____

3. _____

4. _____

5. _____

"You can't give up! If you do, you're like everybody else."

– CHRIS EVERT

30
STOP PEDALING.
ACT NOW.

(DON'T WAIT FOR THE RIGHT TIME, JUST DO IT.)

Do you want to know one thing that drives me absolutely bananas?

People who say, "I'm too busy." Do you hear yourself saying it? People say it to me All. The. Time.

I'm busy, you're busy. Your next-door neighbor, Sandy, is busy, too.

So what? We all get caught up in the busyness of life. (In fact, I've now taken the words "too busy" out of my vocabulary and I now say I'm hard-working.)

If you say you're too busy to do something, that might be code for, "I'm avoiding my goals," or, "I'm using 'busyness' as an excuse because I'm actually afraid of failure."

It's easy to get caught up in the busyness, pedal along and push aside our goals, dreams, values, the people we love, the things we enjoy doing and the places we want to see.

Life is so short. Please, please, *please* don't let life pass you by in a blur.

Spend time planning and reflecting on things you truly want and things that truly matter. By setting goals and achieving them, you will gain confidence. *Confidence and courage breed action.*

I spoke at a conference a few years ago and I'll never forget this particular interaction. A young lady named Lydia raised her hand. She said, "Sonia, I really love what you're saying about goal setting and just *going for it*, but it's just overwhelming for me to figure out how I'm going to reach my goal."

"Lydia, you're a rock star for bringing that up. Tell me, what is your goal?" I asked.

She timidly said (almost as if she were afraid to admit it out loud), "I want to open up my own coffee shop."

"That's brilliant. What have you done so far to get there?"

"Nothing. I'm stuck."

I went on to say, "I've got four suggestions for you so you never, ever lose sight of your coffee shop dream."

Here are the four steps I shared with Lydia:

1. Write down your goal. It makes it more concrete, it makes it more real. Post it where you can see it often—on your bedside table and also by your bathroom mirror so you see it first thing every morning.

2. Write down the steps you're going to take to reach your goal. Read through those every day.

3. Next, tell everyone you know about your goal. If your goal is to open a coffee shop, tell everyone who will listen. *Everyone.* Even strangers in the elevator. Don't listen to the naysayers, either. Nobody can squash your dreams, because, remember, you rock. (Also, it's harder to let yourself down—and everyone else—after you've told them about your goals.)

4. The final step is the most fun. Take one action step *right now.* Right here. For example, if your goal, like Lydia's, is to open up your own coffee shop, google "coffee shop business plans" and start jotting down notes. *Do it! Go! Run! Now.*

Did you do it?

If not, I understand. Fear is a powerful thing. Remember, faking it works—fake it through the fear! Or, think of it this way. What's the smallest effort you could make to overcome your fear and take action toward your goal?

Whatever that step is—do it.

Baby steps. It wasn't that hard, was it?

Nope. Now, repeat.

Again. Then, again.

Each teeny, tiny success makes it easier to have another one.

Remember, a fear that is keeping you from failure could also be keeping you from success.

For some inspiration, take a look at this list of wildly successful people and their list of failures (some are unbelievable!):

- Walt Disney was fired from the *Kansas City Star* newspaper because his editor felt "he lacked imagination and had no good ideas."

- Oprah Winfrey was publicly fired from her first television job for getting too "emotionally invested" in her stories.

- Steven Spielberg was rejected by the University of Southern California School of Cinematic Arts *twice.*

Thomas Edison's teachers told him he was "too stupid to learn anything" and he was fired from his first two employment positions for not being productive enough.

Don't get to the end of your life and wish you had achieved and done more. Do it now.

Just start. Even baby steps count. And remember, fake it—right through your fear!

Write down 5 steps you'll take to reach your goals and take care of one of those steps right this minute.

1. _____

2. _____

3. _____

4. _____

5. _____

"The only person you should try to be better than is the person you were yesterday."

— UNKNOWN

31

BE THE BEST VERSION OF YOU

(IT'S TIME TO BUILD THE BEST SELF YOU CAN BE.)

Introspection. Self-improvement. Dedication to change. Are these a part of your daily (or even weekly) thought processes? Imagine if everyone in the world woke up each morning and asked themselves, "What can I do to make myself a better person today? How can I make someone else feel like a million bucks?"

Each and every day, I try as hard as possible to set my mind to being the best version of me, whilst focusing on my purpose and making a difference. Being me means being *present*. It means focusing on my talents and strengths. It means empowering and inspiring others to be the best versions of themselves. It is about caring and collaborating with those around me and sharing knowledge to help others be better and think differently.

What does being *you* mean?

Maybe it means leading your company with compassion for the people who work for you. Maybe it means teaching a classroom full of students, and each student knows how much you care about them. Maybe it means being a great mum or dad and showing your kids you love them whilst leading by firm example.

I hope you can see how you've morphed and grown from the person who began reading this book. Hopefully, you've taken time to write down your five action steps after each chapter and have given them all some serious thought—and have *taken action* toward them. I hope you've set out to improve yourself—your attitude, your leadership skills, your successes, your vision for your life.

Remember, too, that the best version of yourself should be *your vision*, not anybody else's. Don't waste time and energy trying to be what somebody else wants you to be.

I have a friend, Heather, who spent too much time focused on someone else's vision for her life. Heather's dad, a doctor, expected her to become a doctor, too. He'd always wanted her to take over the family business. She dutifully accepted her role, went to university and took a slew of biology classes. Unhappy after two years in school, she finally cast aside the constricting cocoon she'd built around herself and officially emerged—as a shining example of what it meant to be *her* best self. Heather became an artist and now owns her own extremely successful gallery—and every year, hosts an art auction that raises loads of money for charity.

Check out these other examples:

- Singer Katy Perry's parents raised her as an evangelical Christian (they're both born-again Christians) and didn't approve of her career choice. Apparently, from what I can read, despite her success, they still don't approve. *Unreal.*

- Robert Zemeckis (creator of *Back to the Future* and *Forrest Gump*) had parents who told him he couldn't be a movie director because of his blue collar background. I can't even imagine a world without *Forrest Gump*—and it even won him an Oscar! (Guess he showed 'em!)

- Alfred Nobel, founder of the Nobel Peace Prize, didn't choose science as his first profession. A literature buff and writer, he preferred to write poetry, plays and novels. His father, an inventor and engineer, encouraged him to learn chemical engineering instead. Nobel did create dynamite and over 300 other patents—but made sure that the Nobel Peace Prize also honored excellent writers.

Be fair to yourself. You are unique—*celebrate* that fact!

But—it's not about you all the time, is it? (Knew there was a catch, didn't you?) Be there for others. I've said this before, but isn't that why we've been put on this earth? To help each other?

Being there means doing the clichéd things—holding open doors, smiling at strangers, etc. Think outside the box, though. If you live somewhere cold, scrape the snow off your co-worker's windshield. Acknowledge a homeless person's existence—give him a sandwich. Volunteer at the food shelter. Empower your employees. Show your appreciation by launching your first annual company-wide doughnut day. (Trust me, they'll love you.)

Above all else, be kind.

Be truly passionate about what you do and who you are. Your best version is the only version of the real you. Be the best version of *only* you every single day.

Brainstorm! Write down the ways you can be the *best* version of yourself. I'm adding numbers 1 through 9 here because I *know* you have loads to write down!

1. _____

2. _____

3. _____

4. _____

5. _____

6. _____

7. _____

8. _____

9. _____

"My parents taught me to do whatever makes you happy – follow your bliss. That's why I don't make a lot of movies. I'm very meat and potatoes when it comes to work, putting in eight hours each day. I only do what I love."

— MIKE MYERS

32

JUST ROCK IT!

(WORK IT. ALL THE TIME.)

A few months ago, I had a conversation with someone who has had a long-lasting, wonderful impact on my life. He and I started a deep discussion about how one thought—*just one!*—can spark and change the world forever. (Of course, most of the time, that's not without a lot of hard work added to the mix!)

It didn't take long for us to come up with a very long list of examples, and he and I began firing them at each other, each of us determined to better the other. (Needless to say, it's a very competitive friendship.)

"Gutenberg's printing press," he said.

"The Wright brothers' airplane," I countered.

"Thomas Edison's light bulb."

"Alexander Graham Bell's telephone."

"Berners-Lee's World Wide Web."

I said to my friend, "What if Edison *hadn't* invented the light bulb?"

He laughed and said, "Then someone else would have."

What power does your single thought have? How will you harness it? Rock it? Fake it? *Tackle it?*

On second thought, most of us are bursting with ideas, right? There's not just one thought—*ever*. I know that most of the time, I'm brimming, positively overflowing with ideas and dreams.

Don't let someone else beat you to the punch—you be your own equivalent of Edison, or Alexander Graham Bell. I'm *not* saying you have to be an inventor, by the way—I'm saying, follow your bliss. Do what you love—and when you choose the things you love to do, *launch yourself* toward them. Don't stop until you're happy, satisfied and for heaven's sake, *don't stop until you feel as if your life's work is complete.*

I am always visualising where I want to go and what I want to become. My thoughts and actions are focused wholly on my vision and purpose. Years ago, I really wanted to be one of Australia's Best Leadership Keynote Speakers. At the time, I felt like an imposter and I didn't know if I could do it.

I changed my mindset and reframed it. I said to myself, over and over, *"I am a brilliant keynote speaker,"* and, *"I am going to rock it as a speaker."* I focused on this constantly and also made sure I opened myself up to learning and developing as a speaker, registering with speakers bureaus and speaking at numerous events and conferences across the globe (some for free to gain experience).

Was I nervous? Sure. Did I have to do some power poses? Of course. (Okay, I'll admit it. I had to do a *lot* of power poses.)

But I never once said to myself, *"I can't do this."* I visualised myself on each stage, time and time again, and saw myself rocking it. And today, I truly do see myself as one of the best!

To the leaders I coach, I say, "The brain cannot distinguish between doing and visualising. Think about where you want to be in one, two or ten years and start visualising and acting on it *now!*"

Your thoughts become your actions. What you think, you will produce. Your thoughts have amazing power, but you have to couple your thoughts with *real action.*

No matter what you choose to pursue, I firmly believe that you have the ability to achieve greatness. You do! You have it in you!

On these pages, I've already given you the tools. Use them. Work them. Be confident. And if you're not ...

Fake it. That's right.

You got this. Just rock it!

Now, the most important list of all: Write down how you'll rock it!

1. _____

2. _____

3. _____

4. _____

5. _____

Remember, YOU ROCK!

Book conclusion

Lady Gaga once said, "Don't you ever let a soul in the world tell you that you can't be exactly who you are!"

Thank you for being you. Thank you for being part of the *Just Rock It!* journey. Thank you for having the courage to read this book and answer some important questions about yourself. You truly matter. You are worthy. You are valuable. You are amazing. I believe this book will change mindsets and spark waves of energy amongst individuals around the globe—and you've been a part of that revolution.

My dream is to create a world where we all see the greatness in each other and in ourselves. Imagine a world where we all acknowledge and nurture each other's incredible strengths, dreams and passion within, and we are all out there, rocking it. I'd love then for all of us to look back on our lives and say, "You know what? I lived authentically and had the courage to put myself out there. I didn't care what anyone said or did; I just did it!"

It's your turn. You only have one life. ROCK IT. Start now.

Contact Sonia

If you would like to take your career, life or leadership skills one step further, contact my team at LeadershipHQ to find out how you can get a FREE 30-Minute Just Rock It coaching session!

Also contact me to speak at your next conference, summit or event, as my true passion is speaking all around the world to help everyone be the best they can be, and rock it! It makes my heart sing.

Remember, always and forever, YOU ROCK!

Sonia x

Contacts
www.leadershiphq.com.au
www.soniamcdonald.com.au
info@leadershiphq.com.au
sonia@soniamcdonald.com.au

CPSIA information can be obtained
at www.ICGtesting.com
Printed in the USA
FSHW020504230819
61350FS